heavenly chocolate desserts

heavenly chocolate desserts

tarts, mousses, brownies, and more

RYLAND
PETERS
& SMALL

LONDON NEW YORK

First published in the United States
in 2008 by Ryland Peters & Small, Inc.
519 Broadway, 5th Floor
New York, NY 10012
www.rylandpeters.com

10 9 8 7 6 5 4 3 2 1

Text © Susannah Blake, Tamsin Burnett-
Hall, Maxine Clark, Linda Collister,
Clare Ferguson, Liz Franklin,
Kate Habershon, Rachael Anne Hill,
Jennifer Joyce, Jane Noraika,
Louise Pickford, Sara Jayne Stanes,
Fran Warde, Laura Washburn, and
Ryland Peters & Small 2008

Design and photographs
© Ryland Peters & Small 2008

ISBN 978 1 84597 722 1

**Library of Congress
Cataloging-in-Publication Data**

Heavenly chocolate desserts : tarts,
mousses, brownies, and more / [text,
Susannah Blake ... et al.].
     p. cm.
  Includes index.
  ISBN 978-1-84597-722-1
  1. Cookery (Chocolate) 2. Chocolate
desserts. I. Blake, Susannah.
  TX767.C5H4388 2008
  641.6'374–dc22

2008010133

Printed and bound in China

Editor Céline Hughes

Production Manager Patricia Harrington

Picture Research Emily Westlake

Art Director Leslie Harrington

Publishing Director Alison Starling

Indexer Sandra Shotter

Notes

• All spoon measurements are level
unless otherwise stated.

• Ovens should be preheated to the
specified temperature. Recipes in this
book were tested using a conventional
oven. If using a convection oven, cooking
times should be changed according to the
manufacturer's instructions.

• All eggs are medium, unless otherwise
specified. It is generally recommended
that free-range eggs be used. Recipes
containing raw or partially cooked egg,
or raw fish or shellfish, should not be
served to the very young, very old, anyone
with a compromised immune system, or
pregnant women.

contents

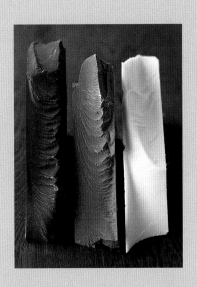

introduction

We've all done it—reached for that chocolate bar when the going gets tough. In fact, for centuries we've known and cherished the mood-enhancing effects of cocoa. So it's no surprise that there's something about a chocolate dessert at the end of a meal that puts a smile on your face and, inexplicably, makes you feel better equipped to deal with life. Whether it's a good old-fashioned brownie with a generous scoop of luxurious vanilla ice cream, a simple chocolate mousse, a suave Sachertorte, or an utterly outrageous pain au chocolat pudding, chocolate is so versatile an ingredient that there are countless ways of serving it up, no matter what mood you're in or what occasion you're catering for.

Just as you should always have flour, eggs, and sugar in your kitchen, ready to whip up a batch of cookies for an impromptu afternoon visitor, make sure you have some fine cooking chocolate in the pantry too. There's nothing like chocolate crèmes brûlées or marbled chocolate cheesecake to butter up a friend or wow your dinner guests.

So whether you're after something sticky, gooey, chilled, creamy, crispy, elegant, naughty, comforting, rich, or smooth, there's a heavenly dessert here to have you licking every last trace of delicious chocolate from your plate (and wishing you'd never invited those people to share it with you).

hot desserts

This luscious crumble is sophisticated enough for the best dinner party. Chocolate and pears were made for each other—here the chocolate melts and mixes with the pear juice to make a delicious sauce. Pumpernickel makes an interestingly crunchy topping, and gives the dessert a dramatic look.

pear and chocolate crumble

2–3 large, not-too-ripe pears

¼ cup superfine sugar

2–3 tablespoons sweetened cocoa powder or grated bittersweet chocolate

finely grated peel of ½ unwaxed lemon

light cream or chocolate ice cream, to serve

choco-pumpernickel topping

4 oz sliced pumpernickel

4 oz stale brown bread

4 tablespoons sweetened cocoa powder or grated bittersweet chocolate

½ stick unsalted butter, chilled

⅓ cup light brown sugar

a medium, shallow, ovenproof dish

SERVES 4

Preheat the oven to 350°F and set a baking sheet on the middle shelf to heat.

Peel, core, and slice (or chop) the pears and put them in the ovenproof dish so that they fill it by two-thirds. Sprinkle the sugar, sweetened cocoa (or grated chocolate, if using), and lemon peel over the top and mix well to coat the pears. Cover and set aside.

To make the topping, tear up the pumpernickel and brown bread and put in the bowl of a food processor. Pulse for a minute or so until very roughly crumbed. Add the sweetened cocoa (or grated chocolate if using), butter, and sugar and pulse again for a minute or so until finer crumbs form. Do not overprocess or it will form a solid lump. Pop in a plastic bag and chill until needed.

When ready to cook the crumble, uncover the pears and sprinkle lightly and evenly with the topping mixture. Place the ovenproof dish on the baking sheet in the preheated oven and bake for 25–30 minutes, or until the pears are very tender and the top nice and crisp.

Remove from the oven and serve warm with light cream or a scoop of chocolate ice cream.

This is a delicious, creamy risotto based on an ancient recipe from the northeast coast of Sicily.
It is variously flavored with vanilla, cinnamon, and chile (a flavor beloved by Sicilians).
A pinch of ground chile in the risotto adds a warmth and mysterious flavor—for adults only.

bittersweet chocolate risotto

3 tablespoons unsweetened cocoa powder

½ cup sugar

¼ teaspoon ground cinnamon

4 cups whole milk

¾ cup risotto rice, preferably *vialone nano*

3 long strips of unwaxed orange peel

3½ oz bittersweet chocolate, grated

½ cup chopped candied orange peel (optional)

to serve

cinnamon sticks

candied orange peel

confectioners' sugar

light cream

4 small bowls or cups, warmed

SERVES 4

Put the cocoa powder, sugar, and cinnamon in a small bowl and add 4 tablespoons of the milk. Mix until well blended, then add another 4 tablespoons of the milk.

Put the rice in a medium saucepan and stir in the cocoa-flavored milk, the remaining milk, and the strips of orange peel. Slowly bring to a boil, then reduce the heat, cover, and barely simmer for 20 minutes. The rice should be very tender, creamy, and slightly sloppy (if not, add a little extra hot milk). Remove the strips of orange peel and stir in the chocolate until it has completely melted, then the candied orange peel, if using.

Spoon into 4 small warm bowls or cups and set a cinnamon stick and a slice of candied peel in each one. Sprinkle with confectioners' sugar and serve immediately with light cream.

This is truly outrageous, and all the better for it! It's probably the most decadent version of classic bread and butter pudding there is, and it is equally at home both as an informal indulgence and as a real dinner party treat. Try using the best *pains au chocolat* you can find, preferably the ones with twin chocolate bars inside. This recipe will even transform the soft supermarket variety into something sublime!

pain au chocolat pudding

4 large *pains au chocolat* (preferably with twin chocolate bars in each)

1¼ cups milk

1¼ cups heavy cream

1 vanilla bean, split lengthwise

4 egg yolks

½ cup plus 2 tablespoons sugar

3½ oz bittersweet chocolate (60–70% cocoa solids), grated (or even chocolate chips)

confectioners' sugar, to dust

light cream, to serve

a 2-quart shallow baking dish, greased

a large roasting pan

SERVES 6

Cut the *pains au chocolat* into thick slices. Arrange the slices, cut-side up and overlapping, in the prepared baking dish.

Put the milk, cream, and vanilla bean in a pan. Cook over very low heat for about 5 minutes, or until the mixture is almost boiling and well flavored with aromatic vanilla. Remove from the heat.

Preheat the oven to 350°F.

In a large bowl, whisk together the egg yolks and caster sugar until light and creamy. Strain the flavored milk through a fine strainer into the egg mixture, whisking well. Whisk in two-thirds of the chocolate. Pour the egg mixture evenly over the *pains au chocolat* and let stand for 10 minutes to allow them to absorb the liquid.

Sprinkle over the remaining chocolate. Put the baking dish in a large roasting pan and pour in enough boiling water to come halfway up the sides of the dish. Bake the pudding for 40–45 minutes, or until the custard is softly set and the top is crisp and golden brown.

Remove from the oven, lift out of the roasting pan, and set aside until just warm. Sprinkle with confectioners' sugar and serve with cream.

This deliciously gooey brownie dessert is an ideal recipe for absolute beginners. If you have suitable oven to tableware it can be made, baked, and served in the same dish so it's a treat for chocolate lovers and dishwashers alike!

brownie lava dessert

½ cup pecan pieces

3½ oz good bittersweet chocolate

1 stick unsalted butter, cubed

1 cup less 1 tablespoon sugar

2 extra-large eggs, lightly beaten

¼ teaspoon pure vanilla extract

½ cup all-purpose flour

light cream or vanilla ice cream, to serve

a flameproof, ovenproof pie dish, approximately 7 inches (across top) and 2½ inches deep

SERVES 4–6

Preheat the oven to 350°F. Put the pecan pieces into a baking dish and lightly toast in the preheated oven for about 10 minutes. Let cool.

Meanwhile break up the chocolate and put it in the flameproof, ovenproof pie dish (or in a medium saucepan). Add the butter and melt gently over very, very low heat, stirring frequently.

Remove from the heat and stir in the sugar, then gradually stir in the eggs followed by the vanilla extract.

When thoroughly mixed, stir in the flour, then finally the nuts. When there are no more floury streaks, scrape down the sides of the dish (if using) so that the mixture doesn't scorch, and put the dish into the preheated oven. Alternatively, if using a pan, transfer the mixture to a greased ovenproof dish.

Bake in the preheated oven for about 30 minutes until the mixture is set on top with a soft gooey layer at the bottom.

Serve immediately with light cream or vanilla ice cream on the side.

pear upside-down dessert

A sophisticated-looking dessert that is really easy to make. Any fresh, ripe fruit can be used, but pears are particularly good.

3 pears, peeled, cored, and halved

6½ tablespoons butter, softened

½ cup natural cane sugar

⅓ cup ground almonds

2 eggs

¾ cup self-rising flour

3 tablespoons cocoa powder

1 teaspoon baking powder

⅓ cup milk

confectioners' sugar, to dust

whipped cream, to serve

a 10-inch tart pan with a removable bottom, greased

SERVES 6

Preheat the oven to 350°F.

Arrange the pears in the bottom of the prepared tart pan. Put the butter and sugar in a bowl and cream until smooth. Add the ground almonds and eggs and beat well. Sift in the flour, cocoa, and baking powder, then fold the mixture together. Add the milk and mix until smooth. Cover the pears with the mixture, smoothing it out with a narrow spatula. Bake in the preheated oven for 25 minutes.

Remove from the oven, let cool for 10 minutes, then turn out onto a plate. Remove the outer ring of the tart pan, and lift off the base by sliding a narrow spatula underneath it. Dust the dessert with confectioners' sugar and serve with whipped cream.

There is nothing better on a cold winter's day than a steamed pudding waiting to be turned out and smothered in sauce. This pudding looks good enough to serve at a dinner party. Smaller oranges are best here, and don't peel them—they are cooked, skins and all, for maximum effect.

chocolate, orange, and date steamed pudding

½ cup sugar

2–3 seedless oranges

1¾ sticks unsalted butter, softened

1 cup dark brown sugar

finely grated peel of
1 unwaxed orange

3 tablespoons fine-cut
orange marmalade

3 eggs, beaten

1 tablespoon orange-flower water
(optional)

1 cup plus 2 tablespoons
all-purpose flour

6 tablespoons unsweetened
cocoa powder

2 teaspoons baking powder

¾ cup pitted dates, chopped

Crème Anglaise (page 145) or
Chocolate Custard Sauce
(page 147), to serve

*a 6-cup pudding mold
(deep heatproof bowl), greased*

SERVES 6–8

First make a sugar syrup. Pour ⅔ cup water into a small saucepan and add the sugar. Cook over gentle heat until dissolved.

Slice each orange thinly into about 6 neat slices. Submerge them in the sugar syrup. Set a disk of nonstick parchment paper on top and simmer gently for 30–40 minutes. Lift the oranges out with a slotted spoon and drain on a wire rack. Boil the syrup until reduced by half.

Line the base of the pudding mold with a disk of nonstick parchment paper. Place the best orange slice on top of the disk, and use the rest of the slices to line the sides of the mold.

In a large bowl, cream the butter, dark brown sugar, and orange peel using an electric mixer, until light and fluffy. Beat in the marmalade, then gradually beat in the eggs and orange-flower water, if using, mixing well between each addition. Sift the flour, cocoa, and baking powder into the egg mixture and fold in. Finally, fold in the dates.

Spoon the mixture into the mold. It should come about three-quarters of the way up the sides. Smooth the surface and cover with a disk of nonstick parchment paper. Take a large sheet of aluminum foil and fold it in half. Make a pleat in the center and place over the mold with the pleat in the center. Press the foil over the side of the mold, tie around the top with kitchen twine, and trim away any excess foil. The pleat will open out and allow the pudding to expand during cooking. Stand the mold on a trivet in a large, deep pan and add enough water to come at least 2 inches up the sides. Cover with a lid and simmer gently for 2 hours, topping up the water level from time to time.

Remove the foil and disk and insert a skewer into the center of the pudding. If it doesn't come out clean, re-cover and steam for a little longer. Run a knife around the sides, turn out onto a dish, and brush with syrup. Serve with Crème Anglaise or Chocolate Custard Sauce.

hot jamaican chocolate bananas

These are a favorite with adults and children, but just leave out the rum if you are serving these to kids. They are really easy to make and can be cooked on the grill, too, so they make a great sweet treat for both winter and summer.

4 firm bananas, peeled

1/4 cup rum (optional)

3 1/2 oz bittersweet chocolate, grated

16 raspberries, to serve

vanilla ice cream or frozen yogurt, to serve

SERVES 4

Preheat the oven to 375°F.

Put each banana on a square of aluminum foil. Pour over the rum, if using, and wrap up to make a package. Put the packages on a baking sheet and bake in the center of the preheated oven for 5 minutes.

Put the chocolate in a small, heatproof bowl set over a small saucepan of steaming but not boiling water and melt gently (do not let the base of the bowl touch the water). Stir occasionally, until smooth.

Remove the bananas from the oven, carefully unwrap the packages, and transfer the bananas to a serving plate or bowl. Add 4 raspberries to each plate, then drizzle the melted chocolate over. Serve immediately with a scoop of ice cream or frozen yogurt.

This is a very simple idea for creating a marvelous special occasion dessert.
Buy the chocolate you most like to eat (there is a huge variety of brands and types available).
Use small saucepans or pretty heatproof bowls set on the table over a warming tray or three
candle-warmers—and have lots of fun.

chocolate fondue

4 oz bittersweet chocolate, chopped

4 oz white chocolate, chopped

4 oz milk chocolate, chopped

2/3 cup heavy cream

1 tablespoon white rum
or Grand Marnier (optional)

to serve

1 small pineapple

2 bananas

4 oz strawberries

4 oz cherries

2 medium pears

*a fondue set, small saucepans,
or heatproof bowls*

SERVES 4–6

Put each type of chocolate into separate small, heatproof bowls set over small saucepans of steaming but not boiling water and melt gently (do not let the base of the bowls touch the water). Stir occasionally, until smooth. Remove the bowls from the heat.

Put the cream into a separate saucepan, bring to a boil, then add 3 tablespoons to each saucepan or bowl of melted chocolate and mix gently. If using white rum or Grand Marnier, add it to the white chocolate mixture.

Set the bowls over the lowest possible heat on a warming tray in the center of the table, surrounded by the fruit. Cut the fruit at the table and immediately dip into the melted chocolate fondues and eat.

These delicious soufflés, with their exceedingly light and meltingly soft texture, are more like hot chocolate mousses. The recipe is easy though—if you can make meringue you can make these soufflés. Serve with crisp cookies for a stunning finale to a special meal.

chocolate soufflés

about 1 tablespoon melted butter

6 oz bittersweet chocolate, chopped

²⁄₃ cup heavy cream

3 extra-large eggs, separated

2 tablespoons Cognac or brandy

2 extra-large egg whites

3 tablespoons sugar,
plus extra for the soufflé dishes

confectioners' sugar, to dust

*4 soufflé dishes, 1 1⁄2 cups each,
or 4 large coffee cups*

SERVES 4

Brush the soufflé dishes with the melted butter, then sprinkle with sugar to give an even coating. Stand the dishes on a baking sheet or in a roasting pan.

Put the chocolate into a medium, heavy saucepan, pour in the cream, then set over very low heat and stir frequently until melted and smooth. Remove from the heat and stir in the egg yolks, one at a time, followed by the Cognac or brandy. At this point the mixture can be covered and set aside for up to 2 hours.

Preheat the oven to 425°F.

Put the 5 egg whites into a spotlessly clean, grease-free bowl and, using an electric mixer, whisk until stiff peaks form. Gradually whisk in the sugar to give a glossy, stiff meringue. The chocolate mixture should feel comfortably warm to your finger, so gently reheat if necessary. Using a large metal spoon, add a little of the meringue to the chocolate mixture and mix thoroughly. This loosens the consistency, making it easier to incorporate the rest of the meringue. Pour the chocolate mixture on top of the remaining meringue and gently fold both mixtures together until just blended.

Spoon the mixture into the prepared soufflé dishes—it should come to just below the rims. Bake in the preheated oven for 8–10 minutes until barely set—the centers should be soft and wobble when gently shaken. Dust with confectioners' sugar and eat immediately.

little hot chocolate mousses

The point of these wonderful desserts is that the center is still blissfully liquid when you serve them, so don't be tempted to cook them for any longer than the stated time. They are delicious served on their own or with ice cream.

5 eggs, plus 5 egg yolks

½ cup sugar

8 oz bittersweet chocolate (60–70% cocoa solids), finely chopped

1¾ sticks unsalted butter

½ cup all-purpose flour

½ cup unsweetened cocoa powder, plus extra to dust

ice cream, to serve (optional)

8 ramekins, greased, or nonstick dariole molds

SERVES 8

Preheat the oven to 350°F.

Put the eggs, egg yolks, and sugar in a large bowl and beat with an electric mixer until the mixture is pale yellow, 10–15 minutes.

Put the chocolate and butter in a heatproof bowl set over a small saucepan of steaming but not boiling water and melt gently (do not let the base of the bowl touch the water). Stir occasionally, until smooth. Remove the bowl from the heat. Add a small amount of the egg and sugar mixture to the melted chocolate and stir until well mixed. Add the rest of the egg mixture and mix well. Sift the flour and cocoa powder into the bowl and gently fold it in with a large metal spoon until just mixed.

Stand the prepared ramekins or molds in a roasting pan and spoon the mixture into them (the mixture should come to just below the rims). Bake on the middle shelf of the preheated oven for 10–12 minutes until risen and just firm to the touch. Don't cook them any longer than this or they will set inside.

Run a round-bladed knife around the inside of each mold to loosen the desserts, then carefully turn them out onto individual plates. Dust with cocoa powder and serve immediately, either on their own or with your favorite ice cream.

An individual white chocolate sponge dessert, baked with a hidden center of molten chocolate and served with cream or Chocolate Fudge Sauce (page 150), is perfect for any occasion. It is very important to use the best white and bittersweet chocolate you can find.

white and black desserts

cream or Chocolate Fudge Sauce
(page 150) (optional)

bittersweet chocolate filling

3 oz bittersweet chocolate, chopped

⅓ cup heavy cream

white chocolate sponge

3½ oz white chocolate, chopped

1½ sticks unsalted butter,
at room temperature

¾ cup sugar

3 extra-large eggs, beaten

1⅔ cups self-rising flour

a pinch of salt

½ teaspoon pure vanilla extract

about ¼ cup milk

an ice cube tray, oiled

*6 small dessert molds,
2¾ inches in diameter, well greased*

SERVES 6

The bittersweet chocolate filling should be made at least 1 hour before making the sponge (though the filling can be kept in the freezer for up to 1 week). Put the chocolate into a heatproof bowl set over a saucepan of steaming but not boiling water and melt gently (do not let the base of the bowl touch the water). Stir occasionally, until smooth. Remove the bowl from the heat, stir in the cream, then pour into the prepared ice cube tray to make 6 "cubes." Freeze for at least 1 hour.

Preheat the oven to 350°F.

When ready to make the desserts, put the white chocolate in a heatproof bowl set over a saucepan of steaming but not boiling water and melt gently (do not let the base of the bowl touch the water). Stir occasionally, until smooth. Remove from the heat, then let cool.

Put the butter into a large bowl and, using a wooden spoon or electric mixer, beat the butter until creamy, then gradually beat in the sugar. When the mixture is very light and fluffy, beat in the eggs, 1 tablespoon at a time, beating well after each addition. Using a large metal spoon, carefully fold in the flour and salt, followed by the melted chocolate, vanilla extract, and just enough milk to give the mixture a firm dropping consistency. Spoon the mixture into the prepared molds to fill by about half. Turn out the bittersweet chocolate cubes, put one into the center of each mold, then top up with more sponge mixture so each one is three-quarters full.

Stand the molds in a roasting pan, then cover loosely with well-buttered foil. Bake in the preheated oven for about 25 minutes or until just firm to the touch. Run a round-bladed knife inside each mold to loosen the desserts, then carefully turn out onto plates. Serve with cream or Chocolate Fudge Sauce, if using.

nutella and bananas on brioche

Children (and adults) around the world are grateful for one of Italy's biggest exports—Nutella. This luxurious chocolate spread made with hazelnuts and chocolate is marvelous just scooped up and devoured by the spoonful. But when warmed up between two pieces of brioche with some banana it becomes something sublime!

4 thick slices of brioche bread

4 tablespoons Nutella or other chocolate-hazelnut spread

1 small banana, peeled and thinly sliced

vegetable oil, for brushing

a panini grill

SERVES 2

Preheat the panini grill.

Spread 2 slices of the brioche with the Nutella. Place the banana slices on top. Close the sandwiches with the second slice of brioche. Brush both sides of the panini with a little oil and toast in the preheated panini grill for 2 minutes, or according to the manufacturer's instructions. The bread should be golden brown and the filling warmed through.

chilled desserts

This amazingly popular dessert is said to have originated in Venice in the 1950s, and it is one that benefits from being made the day before. For added texture, grind real chocolate in a blender for layering and sprinkling. Make this in a large glass dish or in individual glasses for a special occasion.

tiramisù with raspberries

6 oz bittersweet chocolate, (60–70% cocoa solids)

1¼ cups heavy cream

½ cup freshly brewed Italian espresso

6 tablespoons Marsala wine

1 cup mascarpone cheese

⅓ cup sugar

2 tablespoons dark rum

2 egg yolks

24 *savoiardi* biscuits or ladyfingers

1 pint raspberries, plus extra to serve

a serving dish or 4 glasses

SERVES 4 GENEROUSLY

Put the chocolate in a food processor and grind to a powder. Set aside. Pour the cream into a bowl and whisk until soft peaks form. Set aside. Pour the espresso into a second bowl and stir in 2 tablespoons of the Marsala. Set aside. Put the mascarpone in a third bowl and whisk in 3 tablespoons of the sugar, then beat in 2 tablespoons of the Marsala and the rum. Set aside.

To make a zabaglione mixture, put the egg yolks, 2 tablespoons Marsala, and the remaining sugar in a medium heatproof bowl and beat with an electric mixer until well blended. Set over a saucepan of steaming but not boiling water (do not let the base of the bowl touch the water). Whisk the mixture until it is glossy, pale, light, and fluffy and holds a trail when dropped from the whisk. This should take about 5 minutes. Remove from the heat and whisk until cold. Fold in the whipped cream, then fold in the mascarpone mixture.

Dip the *savoiardi*, one at a time, into the espresso mixture. Do not leave them in for too long or they will disintegrate. Start assembling the tiramisù by arranging half the dipped *savoiardi* in the bottom of a serving dish or 4 glasses. Trickle over some of the leftover espresso. Add a layer of raspberries.

Sprinkle with one-third of the ground chocolate, then add half the zabaglione-cream-mascarpone mixture. Arrange the remaining *savoiardi* on top, moisten with any remaining espresso, add some more raspberries, and sprinkle with half the remaining chocolate. Finally spoon over the remaining zabaglione-cream-mascarpone and finish with a thick layer of chocolate and extra raspberries. Chill in the refrigerator for at least 3 hours (overnight is better) for the flavors to develop. Serve chilled.

In these magnificent ice-cream creations, hot fudge sauce contrasts with chilly ice cream and bananas. If that wasn't enough, whipped cream, toasted nuts, and a cherry top everything off for a sinful splurge.

banana splits with hot fudge sauce

4 small bananas, peeled

4 scoops each of strawberry, vanilla, and chocolate ice cream

4 maraschino cherries

½ cup shelled pecans, chopped and toasted

hot fudge sauce

3 oz bittersweet chocolate, chopped

¾ cup heavy cream

2 tablespoons butter

¼ cup light corn syrup

1 teaspoon pure vanilla extract

½ cup sugar

whipped cream

1 cup heavy cream

1 tablespoon superfine sugar

1 teaspoon pure vanilla extract

4 banana split dishes

SERVES 4

To make the hot fudge sauce, put the chocolate, cream, and butter in a medium saucepan. When melted, add the corn syrup, vanilla extract, and sugar, stirring constantly over medium heat. When nearly boiling, turn the heat down to low and simmer for 15 minutes without stirring. Let cool for 5 minutes before using.

To make the whipped cream, whisk the double cream with the sugar and vanilla extract and set aside. Cut the bananas in half lengthwise. Take the banana split bowls and put 2 banana halves along the sides of each one. Put one scoop of each flavor of ice cream between the bananas. Top with one spoonful of the whipped cream, a sprinkling of pecans, and a cherry on top. Serve with a small pitcher of the hot fudge sauce to pour over.

These decadent profiteroles contain a surprise (*sorpresa*) inside: little balls of chocolatey, hazelnutty semifreddo, a kind of ice cream which stays soft when frozen.

profiteroles con sorpresa

Hot Fudge Sauce (page 39, but omitting the light corn syrup), to serve

gianduja semifreddo

1 cup blanched, toasted hazelnuts

4 oz bittersweet chocolate (60–70% cocoa solids), chopped

2¾ cups heavy cream

2 eggs, separated

¾ cup plus 2 tablespoons confectioners' sugar

choux pastry

6 tablespoons unsalted butter, cubed

⅔ cup all-purpose flour, sifted twice with a pinch of salt

2–3 eggs, beaten

a 5-cup freezerproof container

3 baking sheets, lined with nonstick parchment paper

SERVES 6

To make the semifreddo, grind the nuts very finely. Put the chocolate into a heatproof bowl set over a saucepan of steaming water and melt gently (do not let the base of the bowl touch the water). Remove the bowl from the heat and stir until just smooth. Put the cream in a bowl and whisk until soft peaks form, then fold in the ground nuts. Put the egg yolks in another bowl with 2 tablespoons of the sugar and whisk until pale and creamy. Put the egg whites in a spotlessly clean, grease-free bowl and whisk until soft peaks form. Add the remaining sugar to the whites, spoonful by spoonful, whisking between each addition, until very thick. Stir the chocolate into the egg yolk mixture. Fold in the cream, then the meringue mixture. Spoon into a freezer container. Freeze for 12 hours until firm. Put a lined baking sheet in the freezer. Take the semifreddo out of the freezer and refrigerate for 10 minutes before scooping into small balls with an ice cream scoop and spacing apart on the frozen baking sheet. Freeze until hard.

Preheat the oven to 400°F.

To make the choux pastry, put the butter and 1 generous cup water in a heavy saucepan and bring slowly to a boil until the butter has melted. As soon as it hits a rolling boil, add all the flour, remove the pan from the heat, and beat with a wooden spoon. It is ready when the mixture leaves the sides of the pan. Let cool slightly, then beat in the eggs, a little at a time, until the mixture is very smooth and shiny. If the eggs are large, it may not be necessary to add all of them. The mixture should just flop off the spoon when you bang it on the side of the pan. Space teaspoons of the mixture apart on the baking sheets and bake in the preheated oven for 20–30 minutes, or until deep golden.

Remove from the oven and split each one almost in two. Return to the oven for 5 minutes. Cool on a wire rack. Put a semifreddo ball in each one, pushing the halves almost together. Pile into a dish and refrigerate for 10 minutes, then pour over the Hot Fudge Sauce and serve.

A truly seductive end to any party, these fruits make for a great finale.
Super easy to make, but remember to make them at least 1 hour in advance.

strawberries and cherries in tricolor chocolate

8 oz strawberries, stalks on

8 oz cherries, stalks on

1 oz milk chocolate, chopped

1 oz white chocolate, chopped

1 oz bittersweet chocolate, chopped

SERVES 4

Divide the strawberries and cherries into 3 equal piles.

Put the milk chocolate in a heatproof bowl set over a small saucepan of steaming but not boiling water and melt gently (do not let the base of the bowl touch the water). Stir occasionally, until smooth, then remove the bowl from the heat.

Take one of the piles of fruit and dip them halfway into the chocolate, leaving the tops and stalks uncoated and visible. Transfer to a sheet of parchment paper to set.

Repeat with the white and bittersweet chocolate and the other 2 piles of fruit. Refrigerate for at least 1 hour.

To serve, peel off the parchment paper and pile the fruit onto a large serving plate.

very rich chocolate brûlées

The smooth chocolate cream in these brûlées can be made up to 2 days ahead, with the crunchy caramel topping added just before serving. You need a really hot broiler or a cook's blowtorch, available from kitchen suppliers for the best mirror-like finish. If you like, the vanilla bean can be replaced with 1 tablespoon dark rum, added to the mixture at the same time as the egg yolks.

2½ cups heavy cream

1 vanilla bean, split lengthwise

10 oz bittersweet chocolate, chopped

4 extra-large egg yolks

½ cup confectioners' sugar, sifted

about ¼ cup sugar, to sprinkle

8 small soufflé dishes or ramekins, ²/3 cup each

SERVES 8

Pour the cream into a heavy saucepan and add the vanilla bean. Heat gently until just too hot for your finger to bear. Cover with a lid and let infuse for about 30 minutes.

Preheat the oven to 350°F.

Lift out the vanilla bean and, using a tip of a knife, scrape the seeds into the cream. Gently reheat the cream, then remove from the heat and stir in the chocolate. When melted and smooth, let cool slightly.

Meanwhile, put the egg yolks and confectioners' sugar into a mixing bowl, beat with a wooden spoon until well blended, then stir in the warm chocolate cream. Pour into the soufflé dishes, then stand the dishes in a roasting pan half-filled with warm water. Cook in the preheated oven for about 30 minutes until just firm. Remove from the roasting pan and let cool, then cover and chill overnight or for up to 48 hours.

When ready to serve, preheat the broiler to maximum and half-fill the roasting pan with ice cubes and water. Sprinkle the tops of the chocolate creams with sugar, then set the soufflé dishes in the ice water (this prevents the chocolate melting) and quickly flash under the broiler or with a blowtorch until the sugar melts and caramelizes. Eat within 1 hour.

white chocolate and raspberry fools

This is a pretty marbled dessert with a luxurious hint of white chocolate—
an ideal quick and indulgent treat after a light evening meal.

1½ oz white chocolate, chopped

1 cup raspberries

¾ cup Greek yogurt

SERVES 2

Put the chocolate in a heatproof bowl set over a small saucepan of steaming but not boiling water and melt gently (do not let the base of the bowl touch the water). Stir occasionally, until smooth, then remove the bowl from the heat.

Reserve 6 raspberries to decorate, then roughly crush the remaining raspberries with a fork.

Mix the Greek yogurt into the melted chocolate, then gently fold in the crushed raspberries to give a marbled effect. Spoon into 2 glasses and decorate with the reserved raspberries. Cover and refrigerate until ready to serve.

This is the sort of dessert French aunties would have made in the kitchen of their country house during the summer vacation. And most respectable aunties would have had special little pots, about the size of espresso cups, solely for this purpose. You can also use regular crème brûlée ramekins. Good-quality chocolate is imperative.

chocolate cream pots

1 cup whole milk

1 cup heavy cream

3½ oz bittersweet chocolate (at least 70% cocoa solids), finely chopped

3 extra-large whole eggs and 2 egg yolks

⅔ cup sugar

6 ramekins or other heatproof containers

a baking dish

SERVES 6

Put the milk and cream in a saucepan. Bring just to a boil and remove from the heat. Stir in the chocolate until melted.

Put the eggs, yolks, and sugar in a large bowl and mix well, but don't whisk until frothy; the finished dish should be smooth on top and whisking too much will make too many bubbles that mar the surface. Pour in the milk mixture and stir gently until just mixed.

Bring a kettle of water to a boil and preheat the oven to 350°F.

Set the ramekins in the baking dish. Ladle the chocolate mixture into each ramekin to fill well. Open the preheated oven, pull out the shelf, and set the baking dish with the ramekins on the shelf. Pour the boiling water into the baking dish to come about two-thirds up the sides of the ramekins. Carefully push the shelf back in.

Cook until just set and still a bit jiggly in the middle, 25–30 minutes. Remove the dish from the oven, let stand for 5 minutes, then remove the ramekins from the water bath. Let cool uncovered. Serve warm or at room temperature.

This is a great dessert to make when you've got some cranberries stashed in the freezer or during the Christmas season when they are fresh. Their fruity sharpness beautifully complements the chocolate. The result is a tempting, deep red compote hidden under a layer of darkest chocolate mousse. This is for adults only!

dracula's delight

cranberry compote

1 cup fresh or frozen cranberries

6 tablespoons sugar

2 tablespoons Cointreau

chocolate mousse

6½ oz bittersweet chocolate (60–70% cocoa solids), chopped

3 tablespoons freshly brewed strong espresso

3 tablespoons unsalted butter, cubed

1½ tablespoons chocolate liqueur

3 extra-large eggs, separated

4 deep glasses or pots

SERVES 4

To make the cranberry compote, put the cranberries in a small pan with a splash of water and the sugar. Bring to a boil and simmer for 5 minutes until all the cranberries have burst and the compote is thick. Stir in the Cointreau, then spoon into the glasses. Let cool.

To make the chocolate mousse, put the chocolate, espresso, and butter in a heatproof bowl set over a small saucepan of steaming but not boiling water and melt gently (do not let the base of the bowl touch the water). Stir occasionally, until smooth, then remove the bowl from the heat. Stir in the liqueur. Stir in the egg yolks while the chocolate mixture is still hot—this will cook them slightly.

Using an electric mixer, whisk the egg whites in a spotlessy clean, grease-free bowl until they form firm peaks. Using a metal spoon, stir a large spoonful of egg whites into the chocolate mixture to loosen it, then gently fold in the rest. Spoon the mousse on top of the cranberry compote. Cover and refrigerate for at least 6 hours or overnight.

For a dinner party, put the fresh raspberry purée in the bottom of attractive wine glasses and pipe the mousse over the top.

white chocolate mousses

4½ oz best white chocolate, chopped, plus ½ oz, finely grated

1½ sheets of leaf gelatin

¼ cup sugar

2 egg whites

1 teaspoon Framboise (optional)

1¼ cups whipping cream, whisked until it starts to thicken

raspberry purée

14 oz raspberries

confectioners' sugar, to taste

6–8 wine glasses or glass dishes

a nonstick baking sheet

SERVES 6–8

Preheat the oven to 325°F.

To make the raspberry purée, put the raspberries in a blender, with confectioners' sugar to taste, and whizz until smooth. If you prefer a smooth result, push the raspberry purée through a fine-mesh nylon strainer to remove the seeds. Divide the purée among the glass dishes.

Put the chocolate in a heatproof bowl set over a small saucepan of steaming but not boiling water and melt gently (do not let the base of the bowl touch the water). Stir occasionally, until smooth. Remove the bowl from the heat and let cool.

Put the gelatin in a small saucepan and cover with cold water. Let soak for 3 minutes until soft, then drain off the water.

Meanwhile, put the sugar on a nonstick baking sheet and heat in the preheated oven for 5 minutes. Put the egg whites and half the warm sugar in a large bowl and whisk with an electric mixer until stiff peaks form. Beat in the remaining sugar until the mixture is shiny and smooth. Whisk in the Framboise, if using.

Heat the softened gelatin over very low heat, swirling the pan, until it dissolves. Add it to the meringue and stir gently with a large metal spoon to mix. Gently fold in the cooled chocolate, then fold in the whisked cream until the mixture is smooth. Finally, stir in the grated chocolate.

Spoon the mousse on top of the puréed fruit. Alternatively, for a special occasion, pipe the mixture from a large pastry bag fitted with a wide, plain tip. Refrigerate for at least 30 minutes before serving.

These white chocolate cases are a bit fiddly to make, but the end result of these creamy, luscious mousses is so divine that it's worth every minute of preparation. They are quite rich, so serve them to guests with a cup of espresso at the end of a light meal.

bittersweet chocolate, prune, and armagnac mousses

5 oz white chocolate, melted and slightly cooled, plus extra shavings to decorate

5 pitted prunes

1 tablespoon Armagnac

2 oz bittersweet chocolate (70–80% cocoa solids)

½ tablespoon butter

1½ tablespoons heavy cream

1 egg, separated

frosted edible flower petals, to decorate (optional)

a thin sheet of perspex

sticky tape

a baking sheet, lined with parchment paper

MAKES 8

Cut out eight 1¼ x 6-inch strips of perspex, coil each one to make a collar, about 1¼ inches in diameter, and secure with sticky tape. Stand the collars on the prepared baking sheet.

Using a teaspoon, coat the inside of each collar with the white chocolate, leaving the top ragged and smeared. Drop a spoonful of chocolate into the bottom of each collar and spread out to form a base. Chill for about 15 minutes, then remove from the refrigerator and add a little more chocolate to any thin patches so that there's a good layer of chocolate all round. Return to the refrigerator and chill for at least 30 minutes.

Put the prunes, Armagnac, and 2 tablespoons water in a food processor and blend to make a smooth purée. Put the bittersweet chocolate in a heatproof bowl set over a small saucepan of steaming but not boiling water and melt gently (do not let the base of the bowl touch the water). Stir occasionally, until smooth. Remove from the heat and stir in the butter until melted, then stir in the prune purée, cream, and egg yolk.

Put the egg white in a spotlessly clean, grease-free bowl and whisk to form stiff peaks. Fold a spoonful into the chocolate mixture, then fold in the remaining egg white, one-third at a time. Carefully spoon about 2 tablespoons of the mousse into the white chocolate cases and refrigerate for at least 2 hours.

To serve, carefully remove the sticky tape and unpeel the perspex collars. Arrange on a serving plate using a spatula and decorate with shavings of white chocolate or frosted edible flower petals, if liked.

For a silky smooth texture, make sure the chocolate, gelatin, and egg yolk mixture is still warm when folded together, before adding the cream.

chocolate marquise

9 oz best bittersweet chocolate (70% cocoa solids), chopped

3 sheets of leaf gelatin

3 egg yolks

2 tablespoons sugar

2 tablespoons brandy (optional)

1¾ cups whipping cream

unsweetened cocoa powder, to dust

light cream, to serve

a sugar thermometer

a nonstick loaf pan, 1 lb, greased and lined with 2 long strips of nonstick parchment paper so the ends hang over the 4 edges of the pan

SERVES 6

Put the chocolate in a heatproof bowl set over a small saucepan of steaming but not boiling water and melt gently (do not let the base of the bowl touch the water). Stir occasionally, until smooth. Remove the bowl from the heat and let cool slightly.

Put the gelatin in a small saucepan and cover with cold water. Let soak for 3 minutes until soft, then drain off the water. Heat the gelatin over very low heat, swirling the pan, until the gelatin dissolves.

Put the egg yolks in a large, heatproof bowl and beat with an electric mixer until pale and creamy.

Put the sugar and ¼ cup water in a small saucepan and heat gently until the sugar has dissolved. Increase the heat and cook for 3 minutes or until the temperature of the water has reached 240°F—check with a sugar thermometer. Gently pour the sugar syrup onto the egg yolks, beating with an electric mixer as you pour, until the mixture becomes thick and creamy. Beat in the brandy, if using. Add half the warm chocolate and stir well with a large metal spoon until well mixed. Gently stir in the remaining chocolate, followed by the warm gelatin.

Put the cream in a bowl and whisk until it starts to thicken. Using a large metal spoon, gently fold the cream into the chocolate mixture. Pour the mixture into the prepared loaf pan, tapping the base gently on the counter so the mixture reaches the corners. Level the top with a knife. Cover and chill overnight in the refrigerator until set.

When ready to serve, gently lift the marquise out of the pan by pulling up on the parchment paper and transfer to a serving plate. Dust with cocoa powder, then cut into thick slices. Serve with a drizzle of cream.

chocolate, coffee, and vanilla bombe

This impressive recipe is for a single, large bombe, but you can just as easily use individual dariole molds instead.

4 egg yolks

2 teaspoons cornstarch

⅓ cup sugar

1¼ cups milk

5 tablespoons freshly brewed espresso

1 teaspoon pure vanilla extract

1 cup whipping cream

3½ oz bittersweet chocolate, chopped

chocolate shavings, to serve

3 freezerproof containers

a 3-cup dessert mold or pudding mold

SERVES 4–6

Whisk together the egg yolks, cornstarch, and sugar until smooth and creamy. Heat the milk in a pan until almost boiling, then gradually whisk into the egg mixture until smooth. Return to the pan and heat very gently, stirring, for 5–10 minutes until you get a thick custard. Pour into a bowl, press plastic wrap onto the surface, and let cool, then refrigerate.

Divide the custard between 3 bowls. Stir the espresso into one and the vanilla extract into another. Whip the cream until thick and just holding in soft peaks, then fold one-third into the coffee custard and one-third into the vanilla custard.

Put the chocolate in a heatproof bowl set over a small saucepan of steaming but not boiling water and melt gently (do not let the base of the bowl touch the water). Stir occasionally, until smooth. Fold into the third bowl of custard. Fold in a little cream to loosen the mixture, then fold in the remaining cream.

Transfer the 3 custards into the individual freezerproof containers and freeze for about 1 hour until beginning to set around the sides. Blend each one in a food processor and return to the freezer for another 30 minutes.

Blend the chocolate ice cream, then scoop into the mold and spread out in an even layer. Cover and freeze for a further hour, then blend the coffee ice cream and spread on top of the chocolate layer. Blend the vanilla ice cream, then gently spread on top. Re-cover and freeze overnight, or until firm.

To serve, dip the mold in hot water briefly, then turn out onto a serving plate. Decorate with chocolate shavings and serve in slices.

mint chocolate chip ice cream

One for the adults, for when they're jealous of the kids' Rocky Road Ice Cream below.

1 quantity Rich Vanilla Ice Cream (page 143)

about 4 oz chocolate-covered mints, frozen

SERVES 4–6

Put the mints in a food processor and zap to a coarse meal. Stir into freshly churned ice cream. Alternatively, churn the ice cream with half the chocolate mints, then stir in the remainder and freeze.

rocky road ice cream

One for the kids, to put a big smile on their faces.

1½ cups mini-marshmallows

a tub of store-bought chocolate ice cream, softened slightly

nut brittle

6 tablespoons sugar

½ cup shelled pecans or almonds, coarsely crushed

peanut or corn oil, for brushing

SERVES 4

To make the nut brittle, put the sugar and 6 tablespoons water in a saucepan, stir well, then bring to a boil over medium heat. Continue boiling until golden brown, then add the crushed nuts. Pour onto a greased baking sheet, let cool, and set. When set, break up the brittle, then crush with a rolling pin.

Stir the nut brittle and marshmallows into the softened ice cream until evenly distributed. Freeze. Serve with extras such as chopped nuts, shaved chocolate, and nut brittle.

Nobody makes pistachio ice cream like the Italians, but this home-style version is fairly authentic. Most supermarkets sell shelled unsalted pistachios—the roasted and salted snack kind aren't suitable for this recipe. Fresh nuts taste best, so use a fresh pack.

pistachio and chocolate ice cream

¾ cup shelled unsalted pistachios

1 cup heavy cream, well chilled

1¼ cups milk

4 extra-large egg yolks

½ cup sugar

3 oz bittersweet chocolate, finely chopped

an ice-cream maker or freezerproof container

SERVES 4–6

Put the pistachios and 3 tablespoons of the cream into a food processor or blender and process to a fine paste, scraping down the sides from time to time. Transfer the paste to a medium, heavy saucepan and stir in the milk. Heat gently until almost boiling, stirring frequently, then remove from the heat, cover, and let infuse for 15–20 minutes.

Put the egg yolks and sugar into a bowl and mix well. Pour in the pistachio milk and stir well. Pour the mixture back into the saucepan. Stir gently over low heat until the mixture thickens—do not let it boil or it will curdle. Remove from the heat, pour into a clean bowl, let cool, then chill thoroughly. Put in a bowl and refrigerate.

When ready to churn, put the rest of the cream into the chilled bowl and, using a whisk, whip until soft peaks form, then stir in the pistachio mixture and the chopped chocolate. Pour into an ice-cream maker and churn until frozen. Eat immediately or store in the freezer. Alternatively, put the mixture into a freezerproof container and freeze, stirring occasionally.

Italian and French *gelaterias* offer splendid, often simple flavor combinations. Chocolate and nuts are particularly delicious, especially if the chocolate is of the high-quality, bitter type. If you have a mortar and pestle, try to pound the nuts and sugar to a very smooth texture—otherwise use an electric coffee grinder or spice grinder in short bursts.

bitter chocolate and hazelnut gelato

½ cup blanched hazelnuts, finely chopped

1 cup vanilla sugar or sugar

⅔ cup whole milk

8 oz bittersweet chocolate (at least 70% cocoa solids), chopped

1 tablespoon corn syrup

1 tablespoon chocolate or hazelnut liqueur or dark rum

1¾ cups cream

crisp wafers or cookies, to serve (optional)

an ice-cream maker or a 1-quart freezerproof container

SERVES 4–6

Put the chopped hazelnuts in a dry skillet and dry-fry over moderate heat, stirring constantly until they darken and smell toasty, about 2–3 minutes (take care, because they burn easily). Pour out onto a plate and let cool.

Put the toasted hazelnuts and ¼ cup of the sugar in a small electric spice grinder or coffee grinder. Grind in brief bursts, to a smooth, speckly powder.

Put the milk, chocolate, and remaining sugar in a saucepan over very gentle heat. Cook until the chocolate melts, stirring constantly, then add the corn syrup and ground sugar and nuts. Remove from the heat, put the pan into a bowl of ice water, and let cool. Stir in the liqueur and cream and cool again.

Pour the prepared mixture into the ice-cream maker and churn for 20–25 minutes or until set. Alternatively, freeze in the container, covered, for 6 hours, beating and whisking it once after 3 hours.

Serve in scoops with crisp wafers or cookies, if using.

chocolate chip cookie ice-cream sandwiches

These wicked sandwiches are guaranteed to be a hit with children and the young-at-heart. Perfect for a summer lunch in the garden.

6 tablespoons unsalted butter, softened

6 tablespoons sugar

6 tablespoons brown sugar, sifted

1 extra-large egg, beaten

1/2 teaspoon pure vanilla extract

1 cup self-rising flour

1/4 cup unsweetened cocoa powder

1/4 teaspoon salt

2/3 cup chocolate chips (bittersweet, milk, or white), or coarsely chopped chocolate

Rich Vanilla Ice Cream (page 143), for filling

several nonstick baking sheets, lightly greased

MAKES ABOUT 6

Preheat the oven to 350°F.

Cream the butter and sugars together until pale and fluffy. Beat in the egg and vanilla extract.

Sift the flour, cocoa, and salt into a bowl, then fold into the egg mixture. Fold in the chocolate chips.

Put 4 heaping tablespoons of the mixture spaced well apart on each baking sheet. Press them down and spread them out using the back of a wet spoon.

Bake in the preheated oven for 12–15 minutes. Remove from the oven, let cool on the baking sheet for 1 minute, then transfer to a wire rack. When cold, use immediately or store in an airtight container for up to 5 days.

To assemble the sandwiches, spread a thick (about 1 inch) layer of ice cream on a cookie, then press a second one on top. Repeat until all the sandwiches are made, then freeze until ready to serve.

tarts & cheesecakes

This rich, indulgent dessert is something of a show-stopper. With a simple crust made from crumbled brownies, and a filling of creamy, moussey white chocolate and coffee, it couldn't be easier to make. Use plain brownies, or ones studded with walnuts.

white chocolate and kahlúa mousse torte

1 lb baked chocolate brownies

8 oz white chocolate, chopped

generous 1/3 cup freshly brewed espresso

2 tablespoons Kahlúa or other coffee liqueur

1 2/3 cups heavy cream

bittersweet chocolate curls, to decorate

a 9-inch springform cake pan, base and sides lined with parchment paper

SERVES 8

Reserve about half of the brownies and carefully cut the remainder into ⅛-inch thick slices, then use to line the sides of the prepared cake pan to a height of about 1½ inches.

Crumble the remaining brownies into smallish chunks and scatter over the base of the pan. Using your fingers, press down gently to make a firm, flat base, then set aside.

Put the white chocolate in a small, heatproof bowl set over a small saucepan of steaming but not boiling water and melt gently (do not let the base of the bowl touch the water). Stir occasionally, until smooth. Remove from the heat and stir in the espresso until smooth and creamy, then stir in the Kahlúa. Let cool for 10 minutes.

Whip the cream until it just stands in peaks, then fold in a couple of spoonfuls of the coffee mixture to loosen it. Continue folding in the coffee mixture a few spoonfuls at a time to make a smooth, creamy mixture. (If it becomes lumpy, break up the lumps very gently using a wire whisk.)

Pour the mixture into the pan to fill the brownie crust, then cover with plastic wrap and chill overnight until set.

Remove the plastic wrap, carefully release the torte from the pan, and peel off the parchment paper. Serve decorated with chocolate curls and cut into slices.

This is wickedly delicious. Use the darkest chocolate you can find and serve in thin slices. The filling is gooey and rich inside—delicious with a spoonful of sour cherry jam and another of cream. If you like you can spread the base of the tart with the jam before pouring in the mixture.

baked darkest chocolate mousse tart

1 recipe Pâte Sucrée (page 157)

chocolate mousse filling

14 oz bittersweet chocolate (60–70% cocoa solids), chopped

1 stick unsalted butter, cubed

5 extra-large eggs, separated

½ cup plus 2 tablespoons sugar

⅔ cup heavy cream, at room temperature

3 tablespoons dark rum (optional)

to serve

confectioners' sugar, to dust

cream, to serve

a 10-inch tart pan with a removable bottom, 1½ inches deep

baking beans

SERVES 8

Bring the pastry dough to room temperature. Preheat the oven to 375°F.

Roll out the dough thinly on a lightly floured work surface, then use to line the tart pan. Prick the base, then chill or freeze for 15 minutes.

Line with aluminum foil and baking beans and bake blind in the preheated oven for 15 minutes. Remove the foil and beans, reduce the heat to 350°F, and return to the oven for 10–15 minutes to dry out and brown. Let cool and remove from the pan, then transfer to a serving platter.

To make the filling, put the chocolate and butter in a heatproof bowl set over a small saucepan of steaming but not boiling water and melt gently (do not let the base of the bowl touch the water). Stir occasionally, until smooth. Remove from the heat and let cool for a minute or so.

Put the egg yolks and sugar in a bowl and whisk with an electric mixer until pale and creamy. Stir the cream and the rum, if using, into the melted chocolate mixture, then quickly fold in the egg yolk mixture. Put the egg whites into a spotlessly clean, grease-free bowl and whisk until soft peaks form. Quickly fold into the chocolate mixture.

Pour into the tart crust and bake for 25 minutes until risen and a bit wobbly. Remove from the oven and let cool—the filling will sink and firm up as it cools. Dust with confectioners' sugar, and serve at room temperature with cream.

This unusual chocolate and almond cookie crust is the perfect foil
for a sharp lemon and almond filling.

lemon and almond tart with a chocolate amaretti crust

8 oz amaretti cookies or
Italian ratafias

2 oz bittersweet chocolate,
grated or chopped

6 tablespoons unsalted butter,
melted

lemon almond filling

4 extra-large eggs

peel and juice from 3 unwaxed
lemons

½ cup plus 2 tablespoons sugar

1 stick unsalted butter, melted

4 oz ground almonds

⅔ cup sour cream or crème fraîche

*a tart pan, 9 inches in diameter,
1 inch deep*

SERVES 6–8

Preheat the oven to 350°F.

Put the amaretti cookies in a food processor and blend until finely
crushed. Add the chocolate and blend again. Pour in the melted butter
and blend until well mixed and coming together.

Put the tart pan on a baking sheet. Press the mixture evenly over the
base and sides of the tart pan (a potato masher and the back of a small
spoon will help). Bake in the preheated oven for 10 minutes. Remove
from the oven and press the puffed-up crust down again.

Beat the eggs in a bowl and whisk in the lemon peel and juice, sugar,
butter, and almonds. Pour into the amaretti crust and bake for about
25 minutes until set and very lightly brown on top.

Let cool, then spread with the sour cream or crème fraîche and serve
in slices at room temperature.

Chocolate lovers in Italy are well served in Piedmont, in the far northwest. The capital city, Turin, is a veritable heaven-on-earth with irresistible pastry shops on every corner. One famous delight are the *gianduiotti*, chocolates made with bittersweet chocolate and toasted hazelnuts. This *torta* also comes from Turin, but other recipes from the region are made with almonds or walnuts and flavored with brandy, rum, or grated orange peel. Use very fresh nuts for the best flavor.

italian chocolate and hazelnut torta

3½ oz shelled hazelnuts

3½ oz plain butter cookies, such as Petit Beurre

3½ oz bittersweet chocolate, chopped

1 extra-large egg plus 1 extra-large egg yolk, both at room temperature

3 tablespoons sugar

5 tablespoons unsalted butter

cocoa powder, to dust

whipped cream or ice cream, to serve

a springform cake pan, 8 inches in diameter, lightly greased and baselined with parchment paper

SERVES 6–8

Preheat the oven to 400°F.

Put the hazelnuts in an ovenproof dish or on a baking sheet and toast in the preheated oven for 5 minutes or until lightly browned (watch them carefully as they will taste bitter if they become too dark). If the hazelnuts still have their papery brown skins, put them in a clean, dry kitchen towel, then gather up the ends and rub the nuts together to remove the skins. Let cool, then chop coarsely.

Put the cookies in a food processor and work until coarse crumbs form. Alternatively, put them in a plastic bag and crush with a rolling pin.

Put the chocolate in a heatproof bowl set over a small saucepan of steaming but not boiling water and melt gently (do not let the base of the bowl touch the water). Stir occasionally, until smooth.

Meanwhile, put the whole egg, egg yolk, and sugar into a bowl and, using an electric mixer, beat vigorously until the mixture is very pale, thick and mousse-like—when the whisk is lifted, a thick ribbon-like trail slowly falls back into the bowl. Heat the butter in a small, heavy saucepan until just bubbling. Pour the hot butter onto the mixture in a thin, steady stream while still whisking at top speed, then whisk in the melted chocolate. Using a large metal spoon, gently fold in the chopped nuts and crushed cookies. Pour the mixture into the prepared cake pan, spreading it gently and evenly. Cover the pan with plastic wrap, then chill for at least 3 hours or overnight, until firm.

To serve, unclip the pan and remove the torta. Set on a serving plate, sprinkle with cocoa, and serve, well chilled, with whipped cream or ice cream. The torta is best eaten within 5 days. Do not freeze.

Bananas, caramel, and chocolate are just one of the world's best combinations—and this uses a lot of bananas! Cutting them up and standing them upright gives a wonderful deep pie that looks amazing. Use nice ripe bananas here. If you want to use fewer bananas, cut them in thick diagonal slices and spread out over the base of the pan in a thinner layer.

banana and chocolate tarte tatin

½ cup sugar

3½ tablespoons unsalted butter

12 medium, ripe bananas

12 oz all-butter puff pastry dough, thawed if frozen

2½ oz bittersweet chocolate (60–70% cocoa solids), finely grated

whipped cream or Crème Anglaise (page 145), to serve

a flameproof cast-iron skillet, heavy cake pan, or Tatin pan, 10 inches in diameter

SERVES 8

Preheat the oven to 375°F.

Put the sugar and butter in the cast-iron skillet, heavy cake pan, or Tatin pan. Place over medium heat and cook, stirring every now and then, until the mixture bubbles and turns into a smooth, rich toffee. It will look very grainy to start with and the butter will look as if it has split away from the sugar, but just keep stirring and it will gradually come together. Remove from the heat.

Cut the bananas into 3 even pieces. Arrange them standing upright in the skillet or pan, packing them together.

Roll out the pastry dough on a lightly floured surface into a rough circle about 11 inches across. Lay the pastry over the bananas and tuck the edges down into the skillet to make the rim of the tart. Prick the top of the pastry here and there with a fork, then bake in the preheated oven for 35–40 minutes, or until risen and golden. Remove the skillet from the oven and let rest for 10 minutes.

Run a sharp knife around the pastry to free the edges. Pour out any caramel liquid that has gathered in the base and reserve. Invert a serving plate over the top of the skillet. Carefully turn skillet and plate over together, then remove the skillet. Pour over the reserved caramel sauce and immediately sprinkle with the grated chocolate and let melt in the residual heat. Serve cut into wedges with whipped cream or Crème Anglaise.

A very simple and elegant tart recipe. The chestnut flavor is subtle but quite pleasant, and it makes the texture much creamier and smoother. This is easily made in advance and kept in the refrigerator until needed (up to 24 hours), but do not serve it chilled; room temperature is ideal.

chocolate chestnut tart

1 recipe Sweet Rich Shortcrust Pastry (page 156)

cocoa powder, to dust

whipped cream or sweetened crème fraîche, to serve

chocolate chestnut filling

4 oz bittersweet chocolate, chopped

3 tablespoons unsalted butter

1 extra-large egg, beaten

¾ cup heavy cream

1 cup sweetened chestnut purée

a tart pan, 9–10 inches in diameter

baking beans

SERVES 8–10

Preheat the oven to 375°F.

Roll out the pastry dough and use to line the tart pan. Prick the base all over with a fork, then chill for 30 minutes. Line the pastry crust with parchment paper, then fill with baking beans. Bake on a baking sheet in the preheated oven for 12–15 minutes. Remove the parchment paper and baking beans and return the crust to the oven for a further 10 minutes to dry out completely. Let cool slightly before filling.

Reduce the oven temperature to 300°F.

Put the chocolate and butter in a heatproof bowl set over a small saucepan of steaming but not boiling water and melt gently (do not let the base of the bowl touch the water). Stir occasionally, until smooth.

Stir in the egg, cream, and chestnut purée and mix just to blend.

Put the tart crust back on a baking sheet and set this on the oven rack, partly pulled out. (If you try to fill the crust and then transfer it to the oven, it will surely spill over the edges and burn.) Pour the chocolate mixture into the tart crust and slide the oven shelf back into place.

Bake in the preheated oven until just set, 20–25 minutes. Let cool to room temperature before serving.

Make these for a special dessert in the summer, when strawberries are in season and at their juicy best. The tartlets beat anything you can buy from the baker or supermarket. Brushing the inside of the tartlet shells with chocolate keeps the crust crisp and adds a new dimension to the traditional strawberry tart.

strawberry chocolate tartlets

1 recipe Sweet Rich Shortcrust Pastry (page 156)

8 oz bittersweet chocolate, chopped

mascarpone filling

1 cup mascarpone cheese

2 tablespoons sugar

1 cup cream cheese or fromage frais

rose water or Grand Marnier, to taste

strawberry topping

12 large, ripe strawberries

red currant jelly, to glaze

a cookie cutter, 4 inches in diameter

12 deep fluted tartlet or brioche pans, 3 inches in diameter

MAKES 12

Bring the pastry dough to room temperature. Preheat the oven to 375°F.

Roll out the pastry dough as thinly as possible on a lightly floured work surface, then cut out 12 circles with the cookie cutter. Use to line just 6 of the tartlet pans. Trim the edges and prick the bases. Then set another pan inside each one—this will weight down the pastry while it is baking. Chill or freeze for 15 minutes. Bake blind in the preheated oven for about 10–12 minutes until golden and set. Remove the inner pans and return the tartlet crusts to the oven to dry out for 5 minutes. Let cool, then remove from the outer pans. Repeat with the remaining pastry dough to make another 6 tartlets.

Put the chocolate in a heatproof bowl set over a small saucepan of steaming but not boiling water and melt gently (do not let the base of the bowl touch the water). Stir occasionally, until smooth. Sprinkle spoonfuls of melted chocolate randomly from a height onto nonstick parchment paper. Let cool until set. Using a pastry brush, brush the remaining melted chocolate over the insides of the tartlets, making sure they are completely covered. Let cool until set.

To make the filling, put the mascarpone and sugar in a bowl and beat until creamy, then beat in the cream cheese. Add rose water to taste.

Spoon this mixture into the tartlets, filling well, then sit a nice fat strawberry on top. Melt the red currant jelly, let cool slightly, then brush over the strawberries and the exposed mascarpone surface. Set aside in a cool place to set.

To serve, break up the set chocolate swirls and push a shard into each tartlet. Serve immediately.

Served warm with luxuriant coffee bean sauce, this is the tart for chocolate and coffee fiends.
Decadent and refined and perfect for the end of a fabulous dinner.

chocolate pecan tart with coffee bean sauce

1 recipe Pâte Sucrée (page 157)

1 egg, beaten, to glaze

cream (optional), to serve

coffee bean sauce

1 vanilla bean, split lengthwise

1¼ cups milk

1 tablespoon finely ground
espresso coffee powder

1 tablespoon sugar

2 egg yolks

2 tablespoons cognac or Armagnac

chocolate filling

4 oz bittersweet chocolate
(60–70% cocoa solids), chopped

4 tablespoons unsalted butter

3 extra-large eggs, beaten

¾ cup pure maple syrup

1 cup shelled pecans

a tart pan, 10 inches in diameter

baking beans

SERVES 6

To make the coffee bean sauce, put the vanilla bean, milk, coffee, and sugar in a saucepan and heat gently. Bring almost to a boil, then set aside to infuse for 15 minutes. Remove the vanilla bean.

Put the egg yolks in a bowl, beat well, then pour the infused milk into the eggs. Mix well and return to the milk pan. Stir with a wooden spoon over gentle heat. When the mixture has thickened so it coats the back of the spoon, pour into a cold bowl, and stir in the cognac. Cover with plastic wrap, let cool, and chill until needed.

Bring the pastry dough to room temperature. Preheat the oven to 375°F.

Roll out the pastry dough thinly on a lightly floured work surface, then use to line the tart pan. Prick the base, then chill or freeze for 15 minutes. Line with aluminum foil and baking beans and bake blind for 15 minutes. Remove the foil and beans, reduce the oven temperature to 350°F, and return to the oven for 10–15 minutes to dry out and brown. Glaze with the beaten egg and return to the oven for 5–10 minutes. Let cool.

Reduce the oven temperature to 325°F. To make the chocolate filling, put the chocolate and butter in a heatproof bowl set over a saucepan of steaming but not boiling water and melt gently (do not let the base of the bowl touch the water). Stir occasionally, until smooth. Put the eggs and maple syrup in a bowl and beat well. Add to the chocolate mixture. Stir well, and keep stirring over low heat until the mixture starts to thicken. Stir in the pecans, then pour into the tart crust. Bake for 35–40 minutes until just set—the filling will still be a bit wobbly. Serve warm with the sauce and cream, if using.

When you crave the gooey texture of brownies, but in a more sophisticated package,
make this divine tart with a walnut and graham cracker crust.

double chocolate brownie tart
with a walnut crust

6 oz graham crackers

1½ cups shelled walnuts

1 stick unsalted butter, melted

brownie filling

4 oz bittersweet chocolate, chopped

1¾ sticks unsalted butter, softened

2 cups sugar

3 extra-large eggs, beaten

1 teaspoon pure vanilla extract

1 cup all-purpose flour

1⅓ cups white chocolate chips

*a deep cake pan, 9 inches square,
baselined with nonstick
parchment paper*

MAKES ABOUT 16 SQUARES

Crush the crackers and walnuts in a food processor, pulsing to keep the crackers and nuts quite coarse. Stir into the melted butter until evenly coated. Before it cools, press evenly into the base and 1¼ inches up the sides of the prepared cake pan (a flat potato masher will help you to do this). Chill for 20 minutes to set the crust before filling.

Preheat the oven to 350°F.

To make the filling, put the chocolate in a heatproof bowl set over a small saucepan of steaming but not boiling water and melt gently (do not let the base of the bowl touch the water). Stir occasionally, until smooth. Put the butter and sugar in a bowl, cream until light and fluffy, then beat in the eggs. Stir in the melted chocolate and vanilla. Fold in the flour, then half the chocolate chips. Spoon into the tart crust and level the top. Sprinkle with the remaining chocolate chips.

Bake for 35 minutes or until a toothpick inserted in the middle reveals fudgy crumbs. Do not overcook.

Let cool in the pan, then turn out and cut into 16 squares.

This is a cheesecake for a buffet party. It bursts with juicy pieces of tangerine, and is very refreshing after a meal. For a really special occasion, try using tangerines or clementines ready-prepared in a liqueur and sugar syrup, available from gourmet stores.

tangerine and chocolate cheesecake

1 stick butter

8 oz chocolate wafers, crushed

swirls of cream, piped chocolate decorations, and tangerine segments half-dipped in chocolate, to decorate

filling

8 unwaxed tangerines (washed thoroughly if you can't find unwaxed)

3 envelopes powdered gelatin

1 lb mascarpone or cream cheese

4 eggs, separated

1 cup sugar

1¼ cups sour cream or crème fraîche

3 tablespoons Cointreau or Grand Marnier

a springform cake pan, 10 inches in diameter, lined with parchment paper

SERVES 12

Melt the butter in a small saucepan over gentle heat, then stir in the wafer crumbs. Press evenly into the base of the prepared cake pan and chill for 30 minutes.

To make the filling, finely grate the peel of 2 of the tangerines and set aside. Squeeze the juice from 4 of the tangerines and pour into a small saucepan. Sprinkle with the gelatin and let sit for 10 minutes. Remove the flesh from the segments of the remaining tangerines and chop coarsely.

Put the mascarpone in a large bowl and, using a wooden spoon or electric mixer, beat until softened, then beat in the egg yolks, ½ cup of the sugar, the sour cream, and liqueur. Heat the gelatin slowly until dissolved, then stir into the cheese mixture. Fold in the tangerine peel and chopped tangerines.

Put the egg whites into a spotlessly clean, grease-free bowl, whisk until stiff peaks form, then gradually whisk in the remaining sugar. Fold into the cheese mixture and spoon into the cake pan. Level the surface and chill for 3–4 hours until set.

Carefully remove the cheesecake from the pan onto a flat serving plate. Decorate with swirls of cream topped with a chocolate decorations and chocolate-dipped tangerine segments.

A wickedly dense cheesecake to serve with the coffee after dinner. It couldn't be any easier to make. You may add any liqueur you like, but rum works particularly well. Serve in thin slices, straight from the refrigerator so that it is as cool and firm as possible.

chocolate macaroon truffle cheesecake

6 tablespoons butter

2 tablespoons brown sugar

8 oz chocolate-coated cookies or chocolate chip cookies, crushed

filling

8 oz bittersweet chocolate (60–70% cocoa solids), chopped

10 oz cream cheese

½ cup brown sugar

¼ cup dark rum

4 oz macaroons, finely crushed

cocoa powder, to dust

a shallow, 9-inch cake pan with a removable bottom

SERVES 6–8

Melt the butter and sugar in a small saucepan over gentle heat. Stir in the cookie crumbs. Press the crumb mixture thinly (you may not have to use it all) over the base of the cake pan and chill until required.

To make the filling, put the chocolate in a heatproof bowl set over a saucepan of steaming but not boiling water and melt gently (do not let the base of the bowl touch the water). Stir occasionally, until smooth.

Put the soft cheese in a large bowl and, using a wooden spoon or electric mixer, beat until softened. Beat in the brown sugar and rum, then stir in the melted chocolate and crushed macaroons. Spoon into the cake pan and level the surface as neatly as possible. Chill for 1–2 hours.

When firm, dust the top with a thin layer of cocoa powder. Carefully remove from the pan (you may like to warm the sides of the pan to release the cheesecake) and set on a large serving plate.

This creamy cheesecake holds rivulets of real raspberry and chocolate sauces in a crisp chocolatey cookie crust. Alternatively, if your time is limited, you could fold fresh raspberries and grated chocolate into the cheese mixture instead of the sauces.

raspberry and chocolate ripple cheesecake

1 stick butter

2 tablespoons brown sugar

8 oz chocolate wafers, finely crushed

filling

12 oz cream cheese

3 eggs, separated

½ cup sugar

1 teaspoon pure vanilla extract

1 cup heavy cream

3 envelopes powdered gelatin

raspberry ripple

8 oz fresh or frozen raspberries

¼ cup sugar

chocolate ripple

2 oz bittersweet chocolate, chopped

2 tablespoons heavy cream

a deep, 8-inch cake pan with a removable bottom, greased and lined with parchment paper

SERVES 8

Melt the butter and sugar in a small saucepan over gentle heat. Stir in the wafer crumbs. Press the crumb mixture evenly over the base and up the sides of the prepared cake pan. Chill for at least 30 minutes.

To make the filling, put the cream cheese in a large bowl and, using a wooden spoon or electric mixer, beat until softened. Beat in the egg yolks and half the sugar, the vanilla extract, and cream.

Put the gelatin and 2 tablespoons water in a small heatproof bowl set over a saucepan of hot water and stir occasionally until the gelatin has dissolved. Keep it warm. To make the raspberry ripple, put the raspberries and sugar in a saucepan, heat gently until the sugar dissolves, then boil for 1 minute until slightly thickened. Press through a strainer and let cool. To make the chocolate ripple, put the chocolate and cream in another saucepan, heat until the chocolate has melted, then stir well and let cool until just warm, but still pourable. Beat the gelatin into the cheese mixture.

Put the egg whites in a spotlessly clean, grease-free bowl and whisk until stiff but not dry. Whisk in the remaining sugar, gradually, spoonful by spoonful, whisking until thick after each addition. Beat 2 spoonfuls of the meringue into the cheese mixture, then quickly fold in the rest. Put small spoonfuls of mixture over the cookie crust so that they join up, then pour the raspberry and chocolate sauces in between the spoonfuls of mixture. Spoon in the remaining cheese mixture and pour again (keep any remaining sauces to serve). Swirl the mixtures together with a skewer to produce a ripple effect. Give the pan a shake to settle the mixture, then chill for about 2–4 hours until set. To serve, remove the cake from the pan and carefully peel off the paper. Serve in thin slices with any extra sauces.

An outrageously rich cheesecake based on the delicious ingredients of tiramisù—coffee, mascarpone, chocolate, coffee liqueur, and rum. A creamy rum and vanilla mixture is marbled through a bittersweet chocolate, coffee, and liqueur combination, then poured onto an amaretti crust and baked.

tiramisù cheesecake

10 oz amaretti cookies or macaroons, crushed

6 tablespoons unsalted butter, melted

filling

1½ lb mascarpone or cream cheese, at room temperature

¾ cup sugar

3 eggs, separated

3 tablespoons flour

2 tablespoons dark rum

½ teaspoon pure vanilla extract

7 oz bittersweet chocolate, chopped

1 tablespoon finely ground espresso coffee powder

3 tablespoons coffee liqueur, such as Tía María

confectioners' sugar, to dust

a springform cake pan, 9 inches in diameter

SERVES 8–10

Stir the cookie crumbs into the melted butter. Spoon the crumb mixture over the base of the cake pan and press evenly over the base and 1¼ inches up the sides with the back of a spoon to form a neat crust. Chill for at least 30 minutes until firm.

Preheat the oven to 400°F.

To make the filling, put the mascarpone in a bowl and, using a wooden spoon or electric mixer, beat until smooth. Add the sugar and beat until smooth, then beat in the egg yolks. Divide the mixture between 2 bowls. Stir the flour, rum, and vanilla extract into one of the bowls.

Put the chocolate in a heatproof bowl set over a small saucepan of steaming but not boiling water and melt gently (do not let the base of the bowl touch the water). Stir occasionally, until smooth. Let cool slightly, then stir in the coffee and liqueur. Stir into the second bowl. Put the egg whites in a spotlessly clean, grease-free bowl, whisk until soft peaks form, then fold half into each cheese mixture.

Spoon alternate mounds of the cheese mixture onto the cookie crust until full. Swirl the mixtures together with a knife to produce a marbled effect (do not overmix). Bake in the preheated oven for 45 minutes until golden brown, but still soft in the center—cover the top if it appears to be overbrowning. Turn the oven off, then leave the cheesecake in the oven with the door ajar to cool completely. Alternatively, transfer the cheesecake to a wire rack and invert a large bowl over the cake so it cools slowly. When cold, chill for several hours before serving. Serve dusted with confectioners' sugar.

This is a very special cheesecake indeed. Make sure that the chocolate and water are melted together—the shock of adding the water later will make the chocolate thicken and be ruined.

chocolate marble cheesecake

1 stick butter

2 tablespoons brown sugar

8 oz chocolate wafers, finely crushed

a little melted butter

4 oz white chocolate, grated and chilled, to decorate

filling

6 oz bittersweet chocolate (60–70% cocoa solids), chopped

1½ lb cream cheese, at room temperature

1¼ cups sugar

1 vanilla bean, split lengthwise, seeds scraped out and set aside, or 1 teaspoon pure vanilla extract

2 extra-large eggs

a 9-inch springform cake pan or deep sandwich pan with a removable bottom

SERVES 10

Preheat the oven to 350°F. Follow the instructions on page 93 to make a chocolate crumb crust. Press the crumb mixture over the base of the cake pan. Bake in the preheated oven for 15 minutes, then remove from the oven, lightly firm down again, and let cool completely. Reduce the oven temperature to 325°F.

When the base is cold, carefully brush the sides of the pan with a little melted butter, then chill until required.

To make the filling, put the chocolate and 2 tablespoons water in a heatproof bowl set over a saucepan of steaming but not boiling water and melt gently (do not let the base of the bowl touch the water). Keep warm.

Put the cheese, sugar, and vanilla seeds, if using, in a large bowl and beat until soft and creamy. Put the eggs and vanilla extract, if using, in a bowl and whisk well. Beat the eggs gradually into the cheese mixture. Pour 1 cup of the mixture into a small pitcher, then pour the remaining mixture into the prepared pan.

Stir the warm bittersweet chocolate into the reserved cheese mixture. Pour the chocolate mixture in a wide zigzag pattern over the surface of the cheesecake, edge to edge. Draw the handle of a thick wooden spoon through the pattern, zigzagging in the opposite direction so the mixtures are marbled together. Do not overwork, or the pattern will be lost. Keep it simple and the edges neat.

Bake for 20–25 minutes, or until the cheesecake starts to puff slightly around the edges but is still very soft in the center. Transfer to a wire rack and loosen the edges with a very thin knife blade. Let cool slowly by putting a large upturned bowl over the cheesecake. When completely cold, chill for at least 3 hours before removing the pan. Spread the sides lightly with a very thin layer of whipped cream. Press the white chocolate around the sides. Cut with a hot knife to serve.

A semifreddo is a dessert that is half frozen to give it a slightly thickened, creamy texture. Ricotta and mascarpone are sweetened, laced with rum and Tía María, and flavored with pulverized Italian coffee and grated bittersweet chocolate to give an interesting texture. You must buy very finely ground espresso coffee, or it will taste gritty!

coffee ricotta semifreddo cheesecake

1½ sticks butter

3 tablespoons brown sugar

12 oz chocolate wafers, finely crushed

4 oz very cold, bittersweet chocolate, to decorate

confectioners' sugar, to dust

whipped cream, to serve (optional)

filling

12 oz ricotta cheese, at room temperature

12 oz mascarpone cheese, at room temperature

1 tablespoon dark rum

3 tablespoons coffee liqueur, such as Tía María

1 teaspoon pure vanilla extract

4 tablespoons confectioners' sugar

8 oz bittersweet chocolate (60–70% cocoa solids), grated

2 tablespoons espresso ground Italian roast coffee

a springform cake pan, 10 inches in diameter, lined with parchment paper

SERVES 6–8

Follow the instructions on page 93 to make a chocolate crumb crust. Press the crumb mixture over the base of the prepared cake pan. (Use a potato masher to flatten the crumb crust evenly.) Chill until required.

To make the filling, strain the ricotta cheese into a bowl, then beat in the mascarpone cheese with a wooden spoon. (Do not attempt to do this in a food processor, otherwise the mixture will be very runny.)

Beat in the rum, liqueur, vanilla extract, and sugar, then fold in the grated chocolate and ground coffee, leaving the mixture streaky. Carefully spoon onto the crumb crust, leaving the surface coarse.

Freeze for about 2 hours until just frozen, not rock solid. The dessert should be only just frozen or very chilled. Transfer to the refrigerator 30 minutes before serving to soften slightly if too firm.

To serve, unmold, remove the paper, and set on a large serving plate. Using a sharp knife, cut through the very cold bittersweet chocolate to make spiky shards, then use to cover the surface of the cheesecake. Dust with confectioners' sugar and serve with whipped cream, if using.

cakes & bakes

An American diner fixture, and an utterly decadent dinner finale, devil's food cake has
a fine-crumbed texture and meringue-like frosting that both melt in the mouth.

devil's food counter cake
with 7-minute frosting

1½ cups boiling water

1 cup unsweetened cocoa powder

4 eggs, at room temperature

1 tablespoon pure vanilla extract

3½ cups cake flour

1 teaspoon salt

1 teaspoon baking soda

2¼ cups sugar

1½ cups unsalted butter, softened

7-minute frosting

1¼ cups sugar

2 egg whites, at room temperature

1½ tablespoons light corn syrup

¼ teaspoon cream of tartar

¼ teaspoon salt

1 teaspoon pure vanilla extract

*3 cake pans, 8 inches in diameter,
or 2 cake pans, 9 inches in diameter*

SERVES 8–10

Preheat the oven to 350°F. Grease the cake pans and line them with
parchment paper. Grease the paper, then dust with flour and shake off
any excess.

Whisk together the boiling water and cocoa in a medium bowl until
smooth. Let cool to room temperature. When it is cool, beat together
the eggs, vanilla extract, and ⅓ cup of the cocoa mixture.

Sift the flour, salt, and baking soda into the bowl of an electric mixer
and stir in the sugar. Mix on low speed for 30 seconds, then add the
softened butter and remaining cocoa liquid. Mix on low speed then
turn up to medium and beat for 1½ minutes. Add the egg mixture in
3 batches, beating each one for 30 seconds. Don't overbeat. Scrape
the batter into the prepared cake pans and smooth the surfaces.

Bake the cakes in the preheated oven for 25–30 minutes or until
a skewer inserted into the center of the cakes comes out clean.
Rotate the cakes halfway through cooking. Let cool in the pans for
10 minutes then turn out onto wire racks, remove the paper, and let
cool completely. Wrap in plastic wrap for up to 2 days before frosting.

To make the frosting, put 6 tablespoons water and all the ingredients
except the vanilla extract in a large glass bowl set over a small
saucepan of steaming but not boiling water (do not let the bottom of
the bowl touch the water). Beat with an electric mixer on high speed
for 7 minutes. Remove from the heat, add the vanilla extract, and beat
for 2 minutes more, until stiff and glossy.

Put one cake on a plate and top with frosting. Place another cake on
top and spread more frosting over. Top with the last cake, if using,
then frost the sides and the top. Use the back of a spoon to create
peaks. The cake keeps, covered, at room temperature, for up to 2 days.

This is one of a family of meringue cakes that take their name from the flavor of buttercream used to fill them. Buttercream can be heavy and a bit fussy, so this is a less traditional version with a simple chocolate ganache, topped with whipped cream.

almond meringue and chocolate layer cake

1¼ cups heavy cream

2 tablespoons sugar

almond meringue rounds

6 extra-large egg whites

¾ cup plus 2 tablespoons sugar

1¼ cups ground almonds

2 tablespoons cornstarch

chocolate ganache

1⅔ cups heavy cream

11 oz bittersweet chocolate, finely chopped, plus extra to grate on top

baking sheets

a pastry bag fitted with a wide tip

SERVES 6–8

Preheat the oven to 250°F. Trace 3 circles, 8 inches in diameter, onto parchment paper and mark the center point. Put the marked paper on baking sheets and set aside.

To make the meringue rounds, put the egg whites and 2 tablespoons of the sugar into a spotlessly clean, grease-free bowl and, using an electric mixer, whisk until firm peaks form. Put the remaining sugar, the ground almonds, and cornstarch in another bowl and mix well. Gently fold the dry ingredients into the beaten whites until blended.

Transfer a third of the meringue into the pastry bag. Starting in the middle of a circle marked on the parchment paper, pipe out a round, in a spiral fashion, until you reach the marked edge. Repeat to make two more rounds. Alternatively, spread the meringue inside the traced circles with a long, thin spatula, taking care to spread in an even layer so it cooks evenly. Tidy the edges. Bake in the preheated oven for 1½–2 hours until firm and dry. Let cool.

To make the ganache, put the cream in a saucepan and bring just to a boil. Remove from the heat and stir in the chocolate until completely melted. Let cool slightly.

To assemble, put one meringue layer on a serving plate. Top with a third of the ganache. Put another meringue on top, add another third of the ganache, then top with the remaining meringue and the remaining chocolate ganache. Refrigerate until the chocolate has completely cooled.

Whip the cream and sugar until firm and spread on top of the final chocolate layer. Grate some chocolate over the top and refrigerate until needed, at least 3 hours or up to 24 hours. Serve chilled.

A plain sponge cake with a big difference—cardamom. Widely used in Scandinavia and South India, this attractive pale green spice with its tiny black seeds has a unique and memorable fragrance. This simple cake is also delicious topped with frosting.

chocolate, almond, and cardamom cake

7 oz bittersweet chocolate, finely chopped

4 extra-large eggs, separated

1 cup sugar

7 tablespoons unsalted butter, very soft

1 cup firmly packed ground almonds

the ground black seeds from 4 cardamom pods

scant ⅔ cup self-rising flour

confectioners' sugar, to dust

whipped cream or ice cream, to serve

a springform cake pan, 8 inches in diameter, greased and baselined with parchment paper

MAKES ONE MEDIUM CAKE

Preheat the oven to 350°F.

Put the chocolate in a heatproof bowl set over a small saucepan of steaming but not boiling water and melt gently (do not let the base of the bowl touch the water). Stir occasionally, until just smooth. Remove from the heat and leave until the chocolate feels just warm. Gently stir in the egg yolks, then the sugar. Work in the butter, then the ground almonds, ground cardamom, and flour.

Put the egg whites into a spotlessly clean, grease-free bowl and, using an electric mixer, whisk until stiff peaks form. Using a large metal spoon, fold the egg whites into the chocolate mixture in 3 batches.

Spoon into the prepared cake pan and bake in the preheated oven for about 1 hour or until the mixture springs back when you press it gently with your finger.

Remove from the oven, carefully turn out onto a wire rack, and let cool. Wrap in aluminum foil, then leave overnight before cutting. Serve dusted with confectioners' sugar and with whipped cream or ice cream. Best eaten within 5 days.

This famous pie hails from the South—it is supposed to look like the thick, dark, muddy waters of the Mississippi delta. It is very easy to make and is perfect to share with family and friends.

mississippi mud pie

crust

8 oz graham crackers

4 tablespoons unsalted butter

2 oz bittersweet chocolate, finely chopped

filling

6 oz bittersweet chocolate, chopped

1½ sticks unsalted butter, cubed

4 extra-large eggs, beaten

½ cup firmly packed light brown sugar

½ cup firmly packed dark brown sugar

1¾ cups heavy cream

chocolate cream

⅔ cup heavy cream, well chilled

3 tablespoons unsweetened cocoa powder

⅓ cup confectioners' sugar

a springform cake pan, 9 inches in diameter, well greased

SERVES 8

Preheat the oven to 350°F.

To make the crust, put the crackers into a food processor and process until fine crumbs form. Alternatively, put the crackers into a plastic bag and crush with a rolling pin. Transfer the crumbs to a mixing bowl.

Put the butter and chocolate into a heatproof bowl set over a small saucepan of steaming but not boiling water and melt gently (do not let the base of the bowl touch the water). Stir occasionally, until smooth. Remove from the heat, then stir into the cracker crumbs. When well mixed, transfer to the prepared cake pan and, using the back of a spoon, press onto the base and about halfway up the sides of the pan. Chill while making the filling.

To make the filling, melt the chocolate and butter as above. Remove from the heat and let cool.

Put the eggs and sugars into a large mixing bowl and, using an electric mixer, whisk until thick and foamy. Whisk in the cream followed by the melted chocolate. Pour the mixture into the cookie crust and bake in the preheated oven for about 45 minutes until just firm. Let cool for a few minutes, then remove from the pan.

To make the chocolate cream, put the cream into a mixing bowl, then sift the cocoa and confectioners' sugar on top and stir gently with a wooden spoon until blended. Cover and chill for 2 hours.

Serve the pie at room temperature with the chocolate cream. The pie can be made up to 2 days in advance and kept well covered in the refrigerator. Remove from the refrigerator 30 minutes before serving.

You can't beat a classic Black Forest Gateau, and this recipe is the one you want for the ultimate wow-factor. The base is made the traditional way, without flour, for a mouthwateringly light texture.

chocolate cherry cake

9 extra-large eggs, separated

1 cup sugar

1 cup unsweetened cocoa powder

cream and cherry filling

a 25-oz can Morello or Bing cherries in syrup, about 2⅓ cups, plus 3 tablespoons kirsch

scant 2 cups heavy cream

3 tablespoons sugar

2 oz bittersweet chocolate, grated

3 layer cake pans, 8 inches in diameter, greased and baselined with parchment paper

MAKES ONE LARGE CAKE

Preheat the oven to 350°F.

Put the egg yolks and sugar into a bowl and whisk until thick and mousse-like—when the whisk is lifted, a wide, ribbon-like trail will slowly fall back into the bowl. Sift the cocoa onto the mixture and gently fold in with a large metal spoon.

Put the egg whites into a spotlessly clean, grease-free bowl and, using an electric mixer, whisk until stiff peaks form. Carefully fold into the yolk mixture in 3 batches. Pour the mixture into the prepared pans, then bake in the preheated oven for 20–25 minutes until the tops of the cakes spring back when you press them gently. Let cool in the pans before unmolding.

To make the filling, drain the cherries and save the syrup. Leave the cherries on paper towels to drain. Reserve 12 to decorate.

Set one of the cooled sponges on a serving plate and sprinkle 2 tablespoons kirsch syrup over the top.

Put the cream in a bowl and, using an electric mixer, whip until soft peaks form. Sprinkle the sugar over the cream and whip until slightly thicker. Reserve half the cream to cover the cake. Spread half the remaining cream over the bottom layer of sponge. Press half the cherries into the cream.

Sprinkle the second sponge layer with 2 tablespoons kirsch syrup as before, then gently set on top of the first layer. Spread with cream and press in the cherries as before. Top with the last layer of sponge. Sprinkle with 3 tablespoons kirsch syrup. Pipe or spread the top and sides of the cake with the reserved cream, then decorate with the reserved cherries and grated chocolate. Chill until ready to serve. Best eaten within 48 hours.

This dark, moist chocolate cake is made all over southern Italy, but particularly in Capri. Normally it is made with ground almonds, but this recipe has been adapted to suit those who cannot eat nuts—it is equally delicious with a fantastic soft texture.

dark chocolate cake from capri

2½ sticks unsalted butter

8 oz bittersweet chocolate (60–70% cocoa solids), chopped

¼ cup freshly brewed espresso

6 eggs, separated

1 cup sugar

scant ⅓ cup potato flour or cornstarch

½ teaspoon baking powder

1 cup stale white bread crumbs

confectioners' sugar, to dust

whipped cream, to serve

a springform cake pan, 10 inches in diameter, sides well greased, base-lined with nonstick parchment paper

MAKES ONE LARGE CAKE

Preheat the oven to 350°F. Dust the prepared cake pan with flour.

Put the butter and chocolate in a heatproof bowl set over a small saucepan of steaming but not boiling water and melt gently (do not let the base of the bowl touch the water). Stir occasionally, until smooth. Remove from the heat, stir in the coffee, then let cool a little.

Put the egg yolks and half the sugar in a bowl and beat until pale and fluffy. Mix in the potato flour and baking powder. Carefully mix in the chocolate and butter mixture, then fold in the bread crumbs.

Put the egg whites into a spotlessly clean, grease-free bowl and, using an electric mixer, whisk until stiff but not dry, then gradually whisk in the remaining sugar. Gently fold into the mixture. Pour into the prepared cake pan and bake in the preheated oven for about 30 minutes, until risen and almost firm in the center. To test, insert a skewer into the middle of the cake. When removed it should have a little of the mixture clinging to it—this will ensure that the cake is moist. Do not overbake. Invert onto a wire rack to cool, then dust with confectioners' sugar. Serve with whipped cream.

NOTE To make a smaller cake, halve the quantities and bake in an 8-inch cake pan.

Although this recipe contains cream, it doesn't require the butter used in most cakes. The refined white flour is also absent and instead it uses protein-packed almonds. So this is a good choice for a children's birthday cake which won't break too many nutritional rules.

chocolate and raspberry birthday cake

4 eggs

¾ cup unrefined granulated sugar

3½ oz bittersweet chocolate (at least 70% cocoa solids), chopped

1 cup ground almonds

⅔ cup heavy cream or crème fraîche

8–10 oz raspberries

two layer cake pans, 7 inches in diameter, lightly greased and baselined with parchment paper

SERVES 8

Preheat the oven to 350°F.

Put the eggs and sugar in a heatproof bowl and place over a small saucepan of gently simmering water. Whisk with an electric mixer for 5–8 minutes until very thick and creamy. The mixture should leave a trail when it drips from the whisk. Remove the bowl from the saucepan and whisk for 3–5 minutes until cool.

Put the chocolate into a heatproof bowl set over a small saucepan of steaming but not boiling water and melt gently (do not let the base of the bowl touch the water). Stir occasionally, until smooth. Remove from the heat, then let cool.

Gradually add the cooled chocolate to the whisked egg mixture, stirring gently. Stir in the ground almonds, mixing lightly. Divide the mixture evenly between the cake pans and tap each pan lightly on the counter to remove any air bubbles. Bake in the preheated oven for 25–30 minutes until well risen and the tops spring back when touched lightly with your finger. Remove the cakes from the oven and let cool in the pans for about 10 minutes before transferring them to a wire rack to cool completely. The surface will crisp up and crack as it cools. Remove and discard the parchment paper.

Whisk the cream, if using, with an electric mixer until soft peaks form. Spread half the cream or crème fraîche over one layer of the cake and top with half the raspberries. Put the second cake layer on top and decorate with the remaining cream or crème fraîche and raspberries. Store lightly covered in the refrigerator until required. The undecorated cake will keep for 2 days.

The most famous of all the Viennese cakes, this sumptuous chocolate cake was invented in 1832 by the chef at the Hotel Sacher. At the hotel, you can still buy a sachertorte, made from the original recipe and packaged in a stylish wooden box.

sachertorte

6 oz bittersweet chocolate, chopped

1 stick plus 2 tablespoons unsalted butter, at room temperature

3/4 cup sugar

5 extra-large eggs, separated, plus 1 egg white

1 cup all-purpose flour

1/2 teaspoon baking powder

apricot glaze

1/4 cup apricot preserves

1 teaspoon lemon juice

chocolate frosting

1/2 cup heavy cream

6 oz bittersweet chocolate, finely chopped

a little melted milk chocolate, to pipe (optional)

whipped cream, to serve

a 9-inch springform cake pan or one with a removable bottom, greased and baselined with parchment paper

a wax paper pastry bag (optional)

SERVES 12

Preheat the oven to 325°F.

Put the chocolate into a heatproof bowl set over a small saucepan of steaming but not boiling water and melt gently (do not let the base of the bowl touch the water). Stir occasionally, until smooth. Remove from the heat and let cool.

Put the butter in a large bowl and beat until creamy. Add half the sugar and beat until fluffy. Using an electric mixer, beat in the egg yolks, one at a time, beating well after each addition. Stir in the cooled chocolate. Sift the flour and baking powder over and fold in with a metal spoon.

Put the 6 egg whites into a large, spotlessly clean, and grease-free bowl and, using an electric mixer, whisk until stiff peaks form, then beat in the remaining sugar a little at a time. Fold into the chocolate mixture in 3 batches, then spoon into the prepared pan and level the surface. Bake in the preheated oven for 1 hour or until a skewer inserted in the center comes out clean. Let cool in the pan for 10 minutes, then turn out onto a wire rack, remove the lining paper, and let cool.

To make the glaze, put the preserves, lemon juice, and 1 tablespoon water into a saucepan, heat gently, then bring to a boil, stirring constantly. Remove from the heat and strain into a bowl. Brush over the top and sides of the cake. Let cool on the wire rack.

To make the frosting, put the cream into a saucepan and heat until almost boiling. Put the chocolate into a heatproof bowl and pour over the hot cream. Leave for 2 minutes, then stir until smooth and glossy. Put a plate under the wire rack, then pour the frosting over the cake so it covers the top and sides. Let set in a cool place, not the fridge. If liked, put some melted chocolate into a pastry bag and pipe the letter "S" on top of the cake. Serve with whipped cream. Store the cake in an airtight container in a cool place and eat within 1 week.

Use the best chocolate to produce a good flavor. The sponge can be sprinkled with rum and a little rum can also be added to the dark mousse if you like.

chocolate roulade

6 extra-large eggs, separated

1 cup confectioners' sugar, sifted

a heaping ½ cup unsweetened cocoa powder

1–2 tablespoons rum (optional)

grated white chocolate and sifted cocoa powder, to decorate

dark mousse

7 oz bittersweet chocolate, chopped

7 tablespoons unsalted butter, cubed

4 extra-large eggs, separated

1–2 tablespoons rum (optional)

1 tablespoon sugar

white mousse

1¼ cups heavy cream, chilled and whipped

3½ oz best white chocolate, grated

a baking sheet, 12 x 16½ inches, greased and lined with parchment paper

MAKES ONE LARGE CAKE

Preheat the oven to 375°F.

Put the egg yolks and ¾ cup of the confectioners' sugar in a bowl and beat until very light and mousse-like—the whisk should leave a ribbon-like trail when lifted out of the bowl. Sift the cocoa into the bowl and gently fold in with a large metal spoon. Put the egg whites in a spotlessly clean, grease-free bowl and, using an electric mixer, whisk until soft peaks form. Whisk in the remaining confectioners' sugar, 1 tablespoon at a time, until stiff peaks form. Fold into the yolk mixture in 3 batches. Gently spread an even layer of mixture on the prepared baking sheet, then bake in the preheated oven for 8–10 minutes until firm to the touch.

Cover a wire rack with a damp kitchen towel topped with a sheet of parchment paper. Tip the cooked sponge onto the rack, lift off the baking sheet, and peel the paper off the bottom. Let cool.

To make the dark mousse, put the chocolate and butter in a heatproof bowl set over a small saucepan of steaming not boiling water and melt gently. Remove from the heat and gently stir in the egg yolks, then the rum, if using. Let cool. Put the egg whites in a clean bowl, whisk until stiff, then add the sugar and whisk again until stiff. Fold into the chocolate mixture in 3 batches. Chill briefly until just setting.

To make the white mousse, chill the whipped cream if necessary, then fold in the grated chocolate and chill until ready to assemble.

To assemble, sprinkle the sponge with rum, if using. Spread the dark mousse mixture on top, leaving a 1-inch border of sponge all around. Cover with white mousse, then roll up from the narrow end like a jelly roll, using the kitchen towel to help you. Wrap in the kitchen towel to give it a neat shape then chill for 30 minutes–2 hours. When ready to serve, remove the kitchen towel and transfer the roll to a serving plate. Decorate with grated chocolate and cocoa powder.

This is literally a pancake-cake, layered with sweet custard and chocolate and baked in the oven. A wedge of this curious striped chocolate dessert makes a great talking point.

chocolate galette

1½ cups all-purpose flour

½ teaspoon salt

¼ cup sugar

4 eggs

2 cups plus 2 tablespoons milk

4 tablespoons unsalted butter, melted and cooled

2 tablespoons brandy

peanut oil, for brushing

chocolate filling

4 egg yolks

½ cup sugar

2 teaspoons pure vanilla extract

1¼ cups heavy cream

8 oz bittersweet chocolate, grated

7 oz shelled walnuts, finely chopped

a crêpe pan or small skillet, 8 inches in diameter

a springform cake pan, 8 inches in diameter, greased and lined with parchment paper

greased parchment paper

SERVES 8

Preheat the oven to 350°F.

Put the flour into a food processor, add the salt, sugar, eggs, milk, cooled melted butter, and brandy and pulse for a few seconds until smooth. Heat the crêpe pan, brush with peanut oil, then wipe away any excess with a paper towel. Spoon 2 tablespoons of the batter into the hot pan and quickly swirl it around to coat the base of the pan evenly but thinly. If you add too much batter, just tip the extra back into the bowl and trim away the pouring trail. Cook the crêpe for 1 minute, then carefully turn it over and cook the other side. You should have at least 15, depending on how thin you make them.

To make the filling, put the egg yolks and sugar into a bowl and whisk until pale and thick. Beat in the vanilla extract and cream.

Put a crêpe in the base of the prepared cake pan, spread it with a little vanilla cream mixture, and sprinkle with grated chocolate and walnuts. Repeat the layers until you run out of crêpes or fill the pan. Finish with a crêpe and cover it with a piece of greased parchment paper.

Bake in the preheated oven for 30 minutes. Remove from the oven and let cool slightly before unclipping the pan and transferring the galette to a serving plate.

Linzertorte is a classic dish dating back to the glory days of the Austrian Empire, and traditionally made from a nutty shortbread-like pastry and raspberry preserves. This recipe is not authentic, but fresh raspberries are the perfect contrast to the ultra-rich crust.

raspberry and chocolate linzertorte

8 oz shelled hazelnuts

1 stick unsalted butter,
at room temperature

¾ cup confectioners' sugar, sifted,
plus extra to sprinkle

3 extra-large egg yolks

1½ cups all-purpose flour

½ teaspoon baking powder

2 teaspoons ground cinnamon

¼ teaspoon grated nutmeg

¼ cup unsweetened cocoa powder

vanilla ice cream or whipped cream,
to serve

raspberry filling

1½ tablespoons cornstarch

3 tablespoons sugar, or to taste

1¼ lb raspberries

*a 9-inch tart pan with a removable
bottom, well greased*

SERVES 8

Preheat the oven to 350°F.

Put the hazelnuts in an ovenproof dish and toast in the preheated oven for about 15 minutes or until light golden brown. If they still have their papery brown skin, put them in a clean, dry kitchen towel, then gather up the ends and rub the hazelnuts together to loosen the skins. Let cool, then transfer the hazelnuts to a food processor and grind to a fine powder. Keep the oven on.

Put the butter into a mixing bowl and beat until creamy. Add the confectioners' sugar and beat, slowly at first, until fluffy. Beat in the egg yolks one at a time, beating well after each addition. Sift the flour, baking powder, cinnamon, nutmeg, and cocoa onto the mixture and work in using a wooden spoon. Finally, add the ground nuts and work in, using your hands to bring the dough together.

Take three-quarters of the dough and crumble it into the prepared pan. Using your fingers, press the dough over the base and up the sides to cover the inside of the pan completely and form a layer about ½ inch thick. Chill for 15 minutes. Put the remaining dough onto a well floured work surface and roll out, slightly thinner, to a rectangle about 9 x 6 inches. Cut into strips about ½ inch wide.

Sprinkle the cornstarch and sugar over the raspberries and toss gently until almost mixed. Transfer the filling into the pie crust and spread it gently and evenly.

Arrange the lattice strips over the filling—if the dough breaks, just push it back together again. Bake in the preheated oven for about 25–30 minutes, until the dough is a slightly darker brown and just firm. Let cool, then remove from the pan and serve sprinkled with confectioners' sugar. Best eaten the same day. Not suitable for freezing.

Just what you need with ice cream and bananas. If you can take the egg whites out of the fridge for an hour before you start it helps a lot. A wire whisk or electric mixer or whisk and spotlessly clean, grease-free, bowl are essential to beat the whites to a stiff snow.

chocolate meringues

3 oz good bittersweet chocolate, chopped

3 egg whites

a pinch of cream of tartar

¾ cup plus 2 tablespoons sugar

nonstick parchment paper

2 baking sheets

MAKES 12

Preheat the oven to 250°F.

Cut out 2 rectangles of nonstick parchment paper to fit your baking sheets, then put one on each sheet.

Put the chocolate in a heatproof bowl set over a small saucepan of steaming not boiling water and melt gently (do not let the base of the bowl touch the water). Stir occasionally, until smooth. Remove from the heat and let cool slightly while you whisk up the whites.

Put the egg whites and cream of tartar into a large, spotlessly clean, grease-free bowl and, using an electric mixer, whisk until stiff. Tip the sugar onto the whites and whisk until stiff and glossy.

Drizzle the melted chocolate over the meringue then gently stir through, using very few strokes so the mixture looks very streaky and marbled.

Scoop a heaped tablespoon of the mixture out of the bowl and drop onto one of the prepared baking sheets. Repeat with the rest of the mixture to make 12, spacing them slightly apart on the sheets.

Put the meringues in the preheated oven for 2 hours. Remove the baking sheets from the oven and let cool. Peel the meringues off the lining paper and serve. Store in an airtight container for up to 1 week.

These pastry puffs filled with chocolate are a little like the delicious French pastry, *pain au chocolat*. Making them with frozen puff pastry dough is even faster than a trip to the *pâtisserie*. If you prefer, you can use bittersweet chocolate instead of the white.

spiced white chocolate puffs

2 sheets ready-rolled puff pastry
dough, thawed if frozen

all-purpose flour, to dust

6 oz white chocolate,
cut into 24 squares

1 teaspoon apple pie spice

1 egg yolk

2 tablespoons milk

cocoa powder, to dust

MAKES 8

Preheat the oven to 425°F. Grease a baking sheet.

Put the pastry dough on a floured work surface and cut each sheet into 4 pieces, 4 inches square.

Put 3 pieces of chocolate onto each square, then add a light dusting of apple pie spice (use a small tea strainer). Dampen the edges with a little water, then fold them over diagonally to form a triangle. Press the edges together to seal, then, using the blade of a sharp knife, gently tap the sealed edges several times (this will help the pastry rise).

Transfer the triangles to the prepared baking sheet. Put the egg yolk and milk into a small bowl, beat well, then brush over the pastry. Bake in the preheated oven for 10–15 minutes until risen and golden.

Remove from the oven, let cool for 5 minutes, lightly dust with cocoa powder, and serve with coffee.

Some brownie enthusiasts believe that only cocoa should be used, not melted chocolate, as it gives a deeper, truly intense chocolate flavor which balances the sugar necessary to give a proper fudgy texture. Choose the best cocoa you can find.

old-fashioned brownies

1 cup walnut pieces

4 extra-large eggs

1½ cups sugar

1¼ sticks unsalted butter, melted

½ teaspoon pure vanilla extract

1 cup plus 2 tablespoons all-purpose flour

¾ cup unsweetened cocoa powder

a brownie pan, 8 x 10 inches, greased and baselined with parchment paper

MAKES 16

Preheat the oven to 325°F.

Put the walnut pieces in an ovenproof dish and lightly toast in the preheated oven for about 10 minutes. Remove from the oven and let cool. Keep the oven on.

Meanwhile, break the eggs into a mixing bowl. Use an electric mixer to whisk until frothy, then whisk in the sugar. Whisk for a minute then, still whisking constantly, add the melted butter in a steady stream. Whisk for a minute, then whisk in the vanilla extract.

Sieve the flour and cocoa into the bowl and stir in with a wooden spoon. When thoroughly combined stir in the nuts. Transfer the mixture to the prepared pan and spread evenly. Bake in the preheated oven for about 25 minutes until a skewer inserted halfway between the sides and the center comes out just clean. Remove from the oven.

Let cool completely before removing from the pan and cutting into 16 pieces. Store in an airtight container and eat within 5 days.

This recipe is for those seasoned brownie fans who want to try something a bit different. It's really like a fun version of after-dinner mints. You'll need a box (or bar) of bittersweet chocolate with a soft, mint-flavored fondant center, of the type that is most often sold as "after-dinner" mints.

mint brownies

4½ oz good bittersweet chocolate (60–70% cocoa solids), chopped

7 tablespoons unsalted butter, cubed

3 extra-large eggs

1 cup sugar

¾ cup all-purpose flour

2 tablespoons unsweetened cocoa powder

3½–7 oz bittersweet chocolate with mint center (depending on strength of flavor required)

a brownie pan, 8 x 10 inches, greased

MAKES 20

Preheat the oven to 350°F.

Put the chocolate and butter in a heatproof bowl set over a small saucepan of steaming not boiling water and melt gently (do not let the base of the bowl touch the water). Stir occasionally, until smooth. Remove from the heat and let cool.

Whisk the eggs, then add the sugar and whisk until thick and mousse-like. Whisk in the melted chocolate mixture. Sift the flour and cocoa onto the mixture and stir in. When thoroughly combined spoon half the brownie mixture into the prepared pan and spread evenly.

Leave the mint chocolates whole or break them up (depending on the size of the ones you are using). Arrange them over the brownie mixture already in the pan. Spoon the remaining brownie mixture on top and gently spread to cover the chocolate mints.

Bake in the preheated oven for about 25 minutes or until a skewer inserted halfway between the sides and the center comes out just clean (though some of the sticky mint layer will appear). Remove the pan from the oven.

Let cool before removing from the pan and cutting into 20 pieces. Store in an airtight container and eat within 5 days.

Here an easy all-in-one brownie mixture is made thinner and more pliable than usual,
then sliced up and sandwiched with vanilla ice cream. Note that it must be frozen for at least
6 hours before serving.

brownie ice-cream cake

7 oz bittersweet chocolate
(60–70% cocoa solids), chopped

5 tablespoons unsalted butter,
cubed

¾ cup sugar

2 extra-large eggs, lightly beaten

½ teaspoon pure vanilla extract

¾ cup all-purpose flour

½ teaspoon baking powder

⅔ cup finely chopped
toasted almonds

2 pints good vanilla ice cream

Creamy Chocolate Sauce
(page 151), to serve

*a jelly roll pan, 12 x 8 inches, greased
and baselined with parchment paper*

SERVES 8

Preheat the oven to 325°F.

Put the chocolate, butter, and 2 tablespoons water in a heatproof bowl
set over a small saucepan of steaming not boiling water and melt gently
(do not let the base of the bowl touch the water). Stir frequently, until
smooth. Add the sugar and stir well to thoroughly combine. Remove
the bowl from the pan and let cool for a couple of minutes.

Stir in the eggs and vanilla extract and mix well. Sift the flour and
baking powder onto the mixture and mix in. Finally, stir in the nuts.
Transfer the mixture to the prepared pan and spread evenly.

Bake in the preheated oven for about 15–20 minutes or until a skewer
inserted into the center of the mixture comes out just clean. Let cool
completely in the pan, then turn out onto a cutting board.

Cut the brownie in half lengthwise to make 2 long strips. Cut one of
the strips into 8 equal pieces. Wrap the long strip and the 8 top pieces
in foil and freeze until firm. When ready to assemble, transfer the ice
cream to the fridge to slightly soften (it must not be allowed to melt).
Put the long brownie strip onto a freezerproof serving platter or baking
sheet, then pile the ice cream on top and quickly neaten the sides and
top. Arrange the 8 brownie pieces on top. Return to the freezer until
firm then wrap tightly and freeze for at least 6 hours before serving.

When ready to serve, use a sharp knife to cut into 8 portions and offer
a jug of Creamy Chocolate Sauce for pouring. The assembled cake can
be kept in the freezer for up to 1 week.

This attractive blondie—a brownie made with white chocolate—is studded with fresh raspberries and makes a heavenly summer dessert. It is rich but not too heavy. Serve with a fresh raspberry sauce (for example the Melba Sauce on page 155) and vanilla ice cream.

white chocolate and raspberry blondies

9 oz good white chocolate

1¾ sticks unsalted butter, cubed

3 extra-large eggs

¾ cup sugar

½ teaspoon pure vanilla extract

1½ cups all-purpose flour

1 teaspoon baking powder

5 oz raspberries

a brownie pan, 8 inches square, greased and baselined with parchment paper

MAKES 9

Preheat the oven to 350°F.

Break up 5 oz of the chocolate and put it in a heatproof bowl with the butter. Set over a small saucepan of steaming but not boiling water and melt gently (do not let the base of the bowl touch the water). Stir frequently, until smooth. Remove the bowl from the pan and let cool until needed.

Break the eggs into the bowl of an electric mixer or a mixing bowl. Whisk until frothy then add the sugar and vanilla extract and beat thoroughly until very thick and mousse-like.

Whisk in the melted chocolate mixture. Sift the flour and baking powder onto the mixture and fold in. Chop the rest of the chocolate into pieces the size of your little fingernail and stir them in. Spoon the mixture into the prepared pan and spread evenly. Scatter the raspberries over the top.

Bake in the preheated oven for about 25 minutes or until a skewer inserted halfway between the sides and the center comes out just clean. Let cool before removing from the pan and cutting into 9 large pieces. Store in an airtight container and eat within 2 days.

An irresistible combination of crisp phyllo, nuts, and rich bittersweet chocolate makes this dessert a firm favorite at every dinner party. Serve with plenty of whipped cream. For best results, use only the best chocolate and very fresh nuts and, before using the phyllo pastry dough, make sure it has properly thawed, according to the instructions on the package.

nut and chocolate strudel

¾ cup blanched almonds

1 cup shelled unsalted pistachios

1 cup walnut pieces

5 tablespoons unsalted butter

scant ½ cup firmly packed light brown sugar

3 oz bittersweet chocolate

7 oz phyllo pastry dough, thawed if frozen

whipped cream, to serve

cinnamon syrup

½ cup sugar

1 cinnamon stick

1 teaspoon freshly squeezed lemon juice

2 tablespoons clear honey

a large roasting pan, well greased

SERVES 6–8

Preheat the oven to 350°F.

Put all the nuts into a food processor and chop until they resemble coarse bread crumbs. Put the nuts into a heavy, dry skillet and stir over low heat until just starting to color. Because nuts scorch quickly, it's best to undercook slightly, rather than risk overcooking them. Remove from the heat and stir in the butter and sugar. Let cool. Using a sharp knife, chop the chocolate the same size as the chopped nuts, then mix with the nuts.

Unwrap the phyllo pastry dough and put onto a clean work surface. Overlap the sheets to make a large rectangle about 36 x 26 inches.

Sprinkle the filling evenly over the phyllo, then carefully roll up. Arrange in a horseshoe shape in the prepared roasting pan, tucking the ends under neatly. Bake in the preheated oven for about 25 minutes or until the top is crisp and light golden brown. Remove from the oven and let cool in the pan while making the syrup.

To make the syrup, put the sugar and a scant ½ cup water into a medium, heavy saucepan and heat gently, stirring frequently, until dissolved. Bring to a boil, then add the cinnamon stick, lemon juice, and honey and simmer for 10 minutes until syrupy. Let cool for 5 minutes, then remove the cinnamon stick and pour the hot syrup over the strudel. Let cool so the strudel can absorb the syrup, then cut into thick slices and serve with piles of whipped cream. Best eaten within 24 hours. Not suitable for freezing.

This deliciously rich and indulgent chocolate log is hard to resist and creates a tempting sweet treat at Christmas time. For a tasty variation, use canned sweetened chestnut purée for the filling, in place of the whipped cream. Children especially will love this cake, which can be decorated with leaves or holly sprigs, if liked.

bûche de noël

3 eggs

½ cup plus 1 tablespoon sugar, plus extra to sprinkle

⅔ cup all-purpose flour

2 tablespoons unsweetened cocoa powder

1 tablespoon hot water

2¼ cups heavy cream

chocolate frosting

2 oz bittersweet chocolate, chopped

1 stick unsalted butter, softened

1¼ cups confectioners' sugar, sifted, plus extra to dust

1 tablespoon milk

a jelly roll pan, 13 x 9 inches, greased and lined with nonstick parchment paper

SERVES 8–10

Preheat the oven to 400°F.

Put the eggs and sugar in a large bowl. Whisk together using an electric mixer at high speed until the mixture is pale, fluffy, and thick enough to leave a trail on the surface when the whisk is lifted. Sift half the flour and cocoa powder over the mixture and fold it in very gently but thoroughly using a large metal spoon. Sift in the remaining flour and cocoa powder and fold in until evenly mixed. Fold in the water.

Pour the mixture into the prepared pan, tilting it backwards and forwards to spread the mixture evenly. Bake in the preheated oven for 10–12 minutes or until the sponge springs back when lightly pressed.

Turn the cake out onto a sheet of parchment paper sprinkled with superfine sugar and set on a damp kitchen towel. Trim the crusty edges, then roll up the cake from a short side with the paper inside and let cool on a wire rack.

To make the frosting, put the chocolate in a heatproof bowl set over a small saucepan of steaming but not boiling water and melt gently (do not let the base of the bowl touch the water). Stir frequently, until smooth. Beat the butter until pale and fluffy, then gradually stir in the confectioners' sugar. Add the melted chocolate and milk and beat until light and smooth. Whip the cream in another bowl to form stiff peaks.

Unroll the cake, remove the paper, and spread with the whipped cream. Roll it up neatly from a short side and place it on a cake board. Cut a thick diagonal slice off one end and attach it to one side with a little chocolate frosting, to resemble a branch. Spread the remaining frosting evenly over the whole cake, then score the surface with a fork to resemble bark. Chill in the refrigerator, if liked.

on the side

Real vanilla is expensive, but the process that takes it from plant to table is so complex, there is little wonder. Don't be tempted to save money by using cheap, inferior imitation vanilla, the results simply won't be the same. However, do rinse and dry the beans, then bury them deep in a jar of sugar to flavor it in readiness for your next batch of ice cream. There is simply nothing which better complements a chocolate dessert than good vanilla ice cream.

rich vanilla ice cream

2 vanilla beans

1¼ cups whole milk

1¼ cups heavy cream

6 extra-large egg yolks

¾ cup superfine sugar

an ice-cream machine (optional)

SERVES 4–6

Split the vanilla beans lengthwise and scrape out the seeds with the tip of a knife. Put the beans in a saucepan and the seeds in a bowl.

Pour the milk and cream into the saucepan with the vanilla beans and bring just to boiling point. Remove from the heat and set aside to infuse for at least 30 minutes.

Put the eggs and sugar in a bowl and beat until pale and creamy. Return the cream mixture to the heat and bring back to a boil. Pour the hot liquid over the eggs, stir until smooth, then pour back into the pan. Reduce the heat and cook over low heat, stirring constantly with a wooden spoon, until the custard has thickened enough to leave a finger trail on the back of the spoon. Take care that the mixture doesn't overheat and scramble.

Let the custard cool completely, then churn in an ice-cream machine and transfer to a freezerproof container and freeze until ready to serve. Alternatively, to freeze without a machine, put the custard in a shallow, freezerproof container and freeze until almost solid. Remove from the freezer, beat well with a wire whisk or electric mixer until smooth, then return to the freezer. Repeat the process twice more to break down the ice crystals, and the result will be silky ice cream.

NOTE If you have time, the custard will benefit by being left for several hours before churning, to let the flavors develop fully.

This is the ultimate indulgence! Serve drizzled over vanilla ice cream or chocolate brownies.

maple and pecan fudge sauce

5 tablespoons unsalted butter

⅓ cup pure maple syrup

⅓ cup heavy cream

½ cup chopped pecans

SERVES 6–8

Heat the butter, maple syrup, and cream together over low heat until the butter has melted. Increase the heat and simmer fast for 5 minutes, or until the sauce is thick. Stir in the pecans and simmer for a further minute. Let cool for 15–20 minutes and serve warm.

NOTE If you make this sauce in advance and let it cool completely, warm it through before serving.

Crème anglaise or custard sauce should be stirred constantly over very gentle heat otherwise the egg yolks can curdle and spoil the sauce. It is such a versatile sauce that it goes well with a variety of hot and cold chocolate desserts.

crème anglaise

2½ cups milk

1 vanilla bean, split lengthwise

6 egg yolks

2 tablespoons sugar

SERVES 8–10

Put the milk and vanilla bean in a saucepan and set over very gentle heat until it reaches boiling point. Remove from the heat and set aside to infuse for 20 minutes, then discard the vanilla bean.

Whisk the egg yolks and sugar together in a bowl until pale and creamy, then stir in the infused milk. Return to the pan and cook, stirring constantly with a wooden spoon. Do not let the sauce boil.

When the mixture has thickened so that it coats the back of the spoon, remove from the heat. If you plan to serve it cold, cover the surface with plastic wrap to prevent a skin from forming while it cools.

Whisked egg whites are the basis for these crisp tuile baskets. The mixture must be spread thinly, baked until light brown, then quickly draped over an orange to give a basket shape. The tuiles can also be rolled up. Don't worry if the first couple you make are not perfect—you'll soon get the hang of it. Serve them filled with a scoop of ice cream and drizzled with chocolatey sauce.

chocolate baskets

Preheat the oven to 350°F.

Put the egg whites into a spotlessly clean, grease-free bowl and, using an electric mixer, whisk until stiff peaks form. Whisk in the sugar. Sift the flour onto the whites, gently fold it in using a large metal spoon, then fold in the cooled, melted butter, chocolate, and orange peel.

Put a scant tablespoon of the mixture onto a prepared baking sheet and spread thinly with the back of a spoon to make a 5-inch disk. Make another disk in the same way, then bake in the preheated oven for 7–10 minutes until lightly browned. Continue making and baking 2 disks at a time.

Using a spatula, carefully lift each tuile off the baking sheet and, while still hot, drape over an orange so it cools and sets in a basket shape. The hot tuiles can also be rolled around the handle of a wooden spoon to make thin, crisp, rolled-up tubes. If the tuiles become too cool to shape, return them to the oven for 1 minute to soften. Store in an airtight container. Best eaten within 24 hours.

2 extra-large egg whites

½ cup sugar

¼ cup plus 2 tablespoons all-purpose flour

4 tablespoons unsalted butter, melted and cooled

1 oz bittersweet chocolate, very finely chopped

grated peel of 1 unwaxed orange

several baking sheets, lined with nonstick parchment paper

MAKES ABOUT 16

The classic sauce for steamed puddings, such as the wonderful Chocolate, Orange, and Date Steamed Pudding on page 20.

chocolate custard sauce

2 cups milk

3 tablespoons unsweetened cocoa powder

⅓ cup sugar

1 tablespoon cornstarch

2 egg yolks

SERVES 4–6

Put all but 2 tablespoons of the milk into a large, heavy saucepan and heat until almost boiling. Sift the cocoa, sugar, and cornstarch into a heatproof bowl, stir in the egg yolks and the 2 tablespoons cold milk to form a thick paste, then stir in the hot milk. Strain the mixture back into the saucepan and stir constantly over low heat until the mixture thickens—do not let the mixture boil or it will curdle.

Remove from the heat and use immediately, or keep it warm until ready to serve.

Both these cones and wafers are the perfect way to provide an extra dose of chocolate for the truly committed chocolate lover. Simple and endlessly satisfying.

chocolate ice-cream cones

4 oz bittersweet chocolate, chopped

8 ice-cream cones

a pastry brush

several baking sheets, lined with nonstick parchment paper

MAKES 8

Put the chocolate in a heatproof bowl set over a small saucepan of steaming but not boiling water and melt gently (do not let the base of the bowl touch the water). Stir occasionally, until smooth.

Using a pastry brush, brush the inside of the cones with the melted chocolate. Arrange on the baking sheets and let set in a cool place (or the refrigerator in very hot weather).

chocolate ice-cream wafers

1 cup plus 2 tablespoons all-purpose flour

a pinch of salt

½ teaspoon baking powder

scant ¼ cup unsweetened cocoa powder

½ cup sugar

1 stick plus 1 tablespoon unsalted butter, cubed

1 teaspoon pure vanilla extract

several baking sheets, lined with nonstick parchment paper

MAKES 14–16

Preheat the oven to 400°F.

Sift the flour, salt, baking powder, cocoa, and sugar into a food processor. Add the butter and vanilla extract and process until the dough comes together into a ball. Shape into a brick, about 4 x 3 x 2 inches. Wrap in parchment paper and chill until firm. Using a sharp knife, cut the dough into wafer-thin slices. Set apart on the baking sheets and bake in a preheated oven for about 5–7 minutes until just firm and the edges are starting to color. Let cool for 2 minutes until firm enough to transfer to a wire rack.

Best eaten within 5 days. The dough can be kept in the refrigerator for up to 1 week or frozen for up to 1 month.

A lovely thick and rich hot sauce that's not too sweet.

chocolate fudge sauce

6 oz bittersweet chocolate
(60–70% cocoa solids), chopped

3 tablespoons unsalted butter,
cubed

2 tablespoons light corn syrup

¾ cup light cream or half-and-half

SERVES 4–6

Put the chocolate, butter, corn syrup, and cream in a small, heavy pan. Set over low heat and melt gently, stirring constantly. Continue stirring and heating until the mixture is almost at boiling point. Pour into a warm pitcher and serve immediately.

The sauce thickens as it cools but can be gently reheated. Any leftover sauce can be covered and stored in the fridge for up to 2 days. Reheat gently before using.

A deliciously rich sauce and more classic version of the Maple and Pecan Fudge Sauce on page 145.

butterscotch fudge sauce

6 tablespoons unsalted butter,
cubed

1¼ cups firmly packed
light brown sugar

2 tablespoons light corn syrup

½ cup heavy cream

SERVES 6

Put the butter, sugar, and corn syrup in a small, heavy pan. Melt gently over very low heat, stirring frequently, until the sugar dissolves completely (about 10 minutes). When smooth and melted, stir in the cream then raise the heat and stir until the sauce is piping hot but not boiling. Pour into a warm pitcher and serve immediately.

Any leftover sauce can be covered and stored in the fridge for up to 3 days. Reheat gently before using.

A simple yet rich sauce without added sugar—the ideal counterbalance to a particularly sweet dessert or a dollop of the Rich Vanilla Ice Cream on page 143.

creamy chocolate sauce

½ cup heavy cream

3 oz bittersweet chocolate (60–70% cocoa solids), finely chopped

½ teaspoon pure vanilla extract

SERVES 4–6

Pour the cream into a small, heavy saucepan and heat gently, stirring frequently. When it comes to a boil, remove the pan from the heat and let cool for a minute. Stir in the chocolate and vanilla extract and keep stirring until smooth. Pour into a warm pitcher and serve immediately. The sauce thickens as it cools but can be gently reheated.

Any leftover sauce can be covered and stored in the fridge for up to 2 days. Reheat very gently, stirring constantly, before using.

Choose top-quality white chocolate flavored with real vanilla beans (rather than children's bars) for a good rich taste.

white chocolate sauce

7 oz good white chocolate, chopped

1 cup heavy cream

⅓ cup milk

1 vanilla bean, split lengthwise

SERVES 4–6

Put the chocolate in a heatproof bowl set over a small saucepan of steaming but not boiling water and melt gently (do not let the base of the bowl touch the water). Stir frequently, until smooth. Remove the bowl from the pan and let cool until needed.

Put the cream, milk, and vanilla bean into a small, heavy pan. Heat, stirring constantly, until scalding hot but not quite boiling.

Remove from the heat and let stand for 5 minutes. Remove the vanilla bean then pour the hot cream and milk onto the melted chocolate in a thin stream, whisking constantly, until you get make a smooth sauce. Pour into a warm pitcher and serve immediately.

Any leftover sauce can be stored, tightly covered, in the fridge for up to 2 days. Reheat very gently, stirring constantly.

Use good, well-flavored coffee but not espresso (or dilute espresso until it tastes like filter or cafetière coffee).

coffee sauce

3½ oz bittersweet chocolate (60–70% cocoa solids), chopped

4 tablespoons unsalted butter, cubed

½ cup freshly brewed, good coffee

SERVES 4–6

Put the chocolate, butter, and coffee in a heatproof bowl set over a small saucepan of steaming but not boiling water and melt gently (do not let the base of the bowl touch the water). Stir frequently, until smooth. Remove the bowl from the pan. As the sauce cools it will become even thicker. Serve warm.

Any leftover sauce can be stored, tightly covered, in the fridge for up to 2 days. Reheat very gently, stirring constantly.

This tangy passion fruit syrup is sublime poured over vanilla ice cream or fresh fruit pavlova. The sweetest, ripest passion fruit have a very dimpled skin—be sure to buy them like this.

passion fruit sauce

½ cup sugar

⅓ cup passion fruit pulp (from about 6 passion fruit)

SERVES 4

Put the sugar and 6 tablespoons water in a saucepan and heat gently until the sugar dissolves. Add the passion fruit pulp, bring to a boil, then simmer gently for 10 minutes, or until everything is reduced slightly and has thickened. Let cool and serve at room temperature.

In this tempting sauce, fresh blueberries are simmered until they burst and release their juices and luscious flavors. Serve with cream-based desserts such as panna cotta or lemon posset.

blueberry sauce

12 oz blueberries

3 tablespoons sugar

grated peel of ½ unwaxed lemon

a squeeze of fresh lemon juice

SERVES 4

Put the blueberries, sugar, lemon peel, and 1 tablespoon water in a saucepan and heat gently until the sugar dissolves. Increase the heat slightly and simmer, partially covered, for 8–10 minutes, or until the berries soften and the sauce thickens.

Remove from the heat and add the lemon juice. Serve hot or let cool and serve at room temperature.

This fresh raspberry sauce was traditionally served with peaches and cream to make peach Melba, but it is equally delicious with any other fresh fruit, such as strawberries or blueberries. Alternatively, serve it with ice cream or the White Chocolate and Raspberry Blondies on page 135.

melba sauce

8 oz raspberries

2 tablespoons kirsch

1–2 tablespoons confectioners' sugar

SERVES 4–6

Put all the ingredients in a food processor and blend until smooth. Pass the purée through a fine strainer and serve.

Pastry can be made by hand, or in a food processor. If you have cool hands, the hand method is best because more air will be incorporated. If you have hot hands, the food processor is a blessing. The quantities of water added vary according to the humidity of the flour, so always add less than the recipe says—you can add more if the dough is dry.

sweet rich shortcrust pastry

2 cups all-purpose flour

2 tablespoons confectioners' sugar

½ teaspoon salt

1 stick plus 1 tablespoon unsalted butter, chilled and cubed

2 egg yolks

2 tablespoons ice water

MAKES ABOUT 14 OZ DOUGH, ENOUGH TO LINE A TART PAN 10 INCHES IN DIAMETER OR TO MAKE A DOUBLE CRUST FOR A DEEP PIE PLATE 8 INCHES IN DIAMETER

Sift the flour, confectioners' sugar, and salt together into a bowl, then rub in the butter. Mix the egg yolks with the 2 tablespoons ice water. Add to the flour, mixing together lightly with a knife. The dough must have some water in it or it will be too difficult to handle. If it is still too dry, add a little more water, sprinkling it over the flour mixture 1 tablespoon at a time.

Transfer the mixture to a lightly floured work surface. Knead lightly with your hands until smooth. Form the dough into a rough ball. Flatten slightly, then wrap in plastic wrap and chill for at least 30 minutes before rolling out.

This is the classic French sweet pastry dough sometimes known as *pâte sablée* or "sandy pastry," because it has a fine crumbly texture when broken. Its high sugar content means that it can burn very easily—use a timer. It takes slightly longer to blind bake than other pastries—bake at the standard 375°F for 15 minutes, then reduce the temperature to 350°F and cook for a further 10 minutes to dry out completely.

pâte sucrée

1½ cups all-purpose flour

a pinch of salt

¼ cup sugar or confectioners' sugar

6 tablespoons unsalted butter, cubed, at room temperature

2 egg yolks

½ teaspoon pure vanilla extract

2–3 tablespoons ice water

MAKES ABOUT 14 OZ DOUGH, ENOUGH TO LINE A TART PAN 10 INCHES IN DIAMETER OR 6 TARTLET PANS 3 INCHES IN DIAMETER

CLASSIC METHOD Sift the flour, salt, and sugar into a mound on a clean work surface. Make a well in the middle with your fist.

Put the butter, egg yolks, and vanilla extract in the well. Using the fingers of one hand, "peck" the eggs and butter together until the mixture resembles creamy scrambled eggs.

Flick the flour over the egg mixture and chop it through with a spatula or pastry scraper, until it is almost amalgamated but looking very lumpy. Sprinkle with the water and chop again.

Bring together quickly with your hands. Knead lightly into a ball, then flatten slightly. Wrap in plastic wrap, then chill for at least 30 minutes before using. Let return to room temperature before rolling out.

FOOD PROCESSOR METHOD Put the sugar, butter, egg yolks, and vanilla extract in a food processor, then blend until smooth. Add the water and blend again.

Sift the flour and salt onto a sheet of parchment paper, then add to the processor. Blend until just combined. Transfer the dough to a lightly floured work surface. Knead gently until smooth. Form into a flattened ball, then wrap in plastic wrap. Chill or freeze for at least 30 minutes. Let return to room temperature before rolling out. This is quite a delicate dough to roll, so be sure to use enough (but not too much) flour when rolling.

Index

conversion chart

Weights and measures have been rounded up
or down slightly to make measuring easier.

American	Metric	Imperial
6 tbsp butter	85 g	3 oz
7 tbsp butter	100 g	3½ oz
1 stick butter	115 g	4 oz

Volume equivalents:

American	Metric	Imperial
1 teaspoon	5 ml	
1 tablespoon	15 ml	
¼ cup	60 ml	2 fl oz
⅓ cup	75 ml	2½ fl oz
½ cup	125 ml	4 fl oz
⅔ cup	150 ml	5 fl oz (¼ pint)
¾ cup	175 ml	6 fl oz
1 cup	250 ml	8 fl oz

Weight equivalents: **Measurements:**

Imperial	Metric	Inches	cm
1 oz	30 g	¼ inch	5 mm
2 oz	55 g	½ inch	1 cm
3 oz	85 g	1 inch	2.5 cm
3½ oz	100 g	2 inches	5 cm
4 oz	115 g	3 inches	7 cm
6 oz	175 g	4 inches	10 cm
8 oz (½ lb)	225 g	5 inches	12 cm
9 oz	250 g	6 inches	15 cm
10 oz	280 g	7 inches	18 cm
12 oz	350 g	8 inches	20 cm
13 oz	375 g	9 inches	23 cm
14 oz	400 g	10 inches	25 cm
15 oz	425 g	11 inches	28 cm
16 oz (1 lb)	450 g	12 inches	30 cm

Oven temperatures:

120°C	(250°F)	Gas ½
140°C	(275°F)	Gas 1
150°C	(300°F)	Gas 2
170°C	(325°F)	Gas 3
180°C	(350°F)	Gas 4
190°C	(375°F)	Gas 5
200°C	(400°F)	Gas 6

Recipe Credits

SUSANNAH BLAKE
Bittersweet chocolate, prune, and
armagnac mousses
Chocolate, coffee, and vanilla
bombe
White chocolate and Kahlúa mousse
torte

TAMSIN BURNETT-HALL
White chocolate and raspberry fools

MAXINE CLARK
Pear and chocolate crumble
Bittersweet chocolate risotto
Pain au chocolat pudding
Chocolate, orange, and date
steamed pudding
Dracula's delight
Banana and chocolate tarte Tatin
Tiramisù with raspberries
Profiteroles con sorpresa
Baked darkest chocolate mousse tart
Lemon and almond tart with a
chocolate amaretti crust
Strawberry chocolate tartlets
Chocolate pecan tart with coffee
bean sauce
Double chocolate brownie tart with
a walnut crust
Pâte sucrée
Sweet rich shortcrust pastry
Tangerine and chocolate cheesecake

Chocolate macaroon truffle
cheesecake
Raspberry and chocolate ripple
cheesecake
Tiramisù cheesecake
Chocolate marble cheesecake
Coffee ricotta semifreddo
cheesecake
Dark chocolate cake from Capri

LINDA COLLISTER
Brownie lava dessert
Old-fashioned brownies
Mint brownies
Brownie ice-cream cake
White chocolate and raspberry
blondies
Chocolate fudge sauce
Butterscotch fudge sauce
Creamy chocolate sauce
White chocolate sauce
Coffee sauce
Chocolate fondue
Chocolate soufflés
Very rich chocolate brûlées
White and black desserts
Pistachio and chocolate ice cream
Italian chocolate and hazelnut torta
Mississippi mud pie
Sachertorte
Raspberry and chocolate linzertorte
Nut and chocolate strudel

Chocolate baskets
Chocolate custard sauce
Chocolate ice-cream wafers
Chocolate ice-cream cones
Chocolate, almond, and
cardamom cake
Chocolate cherry cake
Chocolate roulade
Chocolate meringues

CLARE FERGUSON
Bitter chocolate and hazelnut gelato

LIZ FRANKLIN
Rich vanilla ice cream

KATE HABERSHON
Chocolate galette

RACHAEL ANNE HILL
Hot Jamaican chocolate bananas
Chocolate and raspberry birthday
cake

JENNIFER JOYCE
Nutella and bananas on brioche
Banana splits with hot fudge sauce
Devil's food counter cake with
7-minute frosting

JANE NORAIKA
Strawberries and cherries in tricolor
chocolate

ELSA PETERSEN-SCHEPELERN
Rocky road ice cream
Mint chocolate chip ice cream
Chocolate chip cookie ice-cream
sandwiches

LOUISE PICKFORD
Spiced white chocolate puffs
Crème anglaise
Maple and pecan fudge sauce
Blueberry sauce
Melba sauce
Passion fruit sauce

ANNE SHEASBY
Bûche de Noël

SARA JAYNE STANES
Little hot chocolate mousses
White chocolate mousses
Chocolate marquise

FRAN WARDE
Pear upside-down dessert

LAURA WASHBURN
Chocolate cream pots
Chocolate chestnut tart
Almond meringue and chocolate
layer cake

Photography Credits

CAROLINE ARBER
Page 8ac, 19

MARTIN BRIGDALE
Pages 8ar, bc & br, 13, 24, 27, 31, 34al, cl, c, &
bc, 37, 38, 41, 44, 48, 54, 58, 63, 65, 68a & b all,
cl &cr, 70, 73, 75, 76, 81, 82, 85, 87, 88, 91, 92,
95, 97, 98, 101ac, cl & cr, 102, 105, 109, 117,
123, 137, 138, 140ac, c, cr & bc, 146, 147, 148,
149, 156, 157

PETER CASSIDY
Endpapers, pages 1, 4-5a, 5, 8al & c, 10, 14, 21,
34bl, 50, 68c, 78, 127

JEAN CAZALS
Page 101ar, 112

NICKI DOWEY
Page 22

RICHARD JUNG
Pages 2, 3, 6, 7, 8cl & cr, 16, 29, 34ar, 53, 57,
101bc & br, 128, 131, 133, 134, 140al & ar,
151, 153

WILLIAM LINGWOOD
Pages 42, 120, 140cl, 142

NOEL MURPHY
Page 114

WILLIAM REAVELL
Pages 8bl, 32, 34ac, 47

DEBI TRELOAR
Pages 34cr & br, 60, 66, 101ar, c& br, 106,
111, 119

IAN WALLACE
Pages 140bl & br, 144, 154

POLLY WREFORD
Page 124